Private Pilot Airman Knowledge Test Question Bank

The charts, tables, and graphs used in this publication are for illustration purposes only and cannot be used for navigation or to determine actual aircraft performance.

All rights reserved. No part of this publication may be reproduced, stored in a retrieval system, or transmitted in any form or by any means, electronic, mechanical, photocopying, recording, or otherwise, without the prior permission of the publisher.

ISBN-13: 978-0-88487-535-2
ISBN-10: 0-88487-535-0

Jeppesen
55 Inverness Dr. East
Englewood, CO 80112-5498
Web Site: www.jeppesen.com
Email: Captain@jeppesen.com
Copyright © Jeppesen
All Rights Reserved. Published 1992-2009
Printed in the United States of America

10001343-016

CONTENTS

	Page
Latest Information Regarding Airman Knowledge Tests	iii
Preface	iv
Private Pilot Airman Knowledge Test Question Bank	1
APPENDIX A Learning Statement Codes and Learning Statements	A-1
APPENDIX B Exams and Answer Keys	B-1

Latest Information Regarding Airman Knowledge Tests

The FAA continues to be concerned that many students are memorizing the position of the correct answers on the FAA knowledge tests. Because of this, they regularly change the order of the answer choices to most questions in their knowledge test databases. This means that if you learn the answer to a question based on the letter of the correct answer or its position below the question, you will likely answer the question incorrectly. Because the FAA changes the sequence of the answer choices on a regular basis, it is impossible for test preparation courses to match the answer sequence as it appears on the test.

In addition, the FAA now publishes only selected questions from their database, limiting the number of questions available to the public. Therefore, you might see questions on your knowledge test that are worded differently than those in this guide. This Jeppesen question bank contains the questions published on the FAA web site plus additional questions that should help you pass your airman knowledge test. If are able to answer the questions in this guide, then you can reasonably expect to have the required knowledge to pass the FAA Knowledge Test.

Jeppesen has never encouraged its students to memorize answers to FAA questions. We provide comprehensive, no-nonsense study material that teaches you what you need to know to answer the test questions correctly. Our test prep materials always tell you why the correct answer is correct and, if it is not obvious, why the other answers are incorrect. We want you to know the material, not memorize it.

When answering each FAA question, carefully read and evaluate each answer choice and choose the correct answer based on what you know from your study, not from that answer's position.

Preface

This Private Pilot Airman Knowledge Test Question Bank is designed to help you prepare for the Private Pilot computerized test. It is appropriate for use with several components and options from the Jeppesen Guided Flight Discovery (GFD) Training System, including the Jeppesen Computerized Testing Supplement for Recreational Pilot and Private Pilot.

This question bank includes FAA questions for Recreational Pilot and Private Pilot knowledge tests. It can be used to prepare for the following FAA tests:

> Recreational Pilot — Airplane (RPA)
> Recreational Pilot — Helicopter (RPH)
> Private Pilot — Airplane/Recreational Pilot — Transition (PAT)
> Private Pilot — Helicopter/Recreational Pilot — Transition (PHT)
> Private Pilot — Airplane (PAR)
> Private Pilot — Rotorcraft/Helicopter (PRH)

HOW TO PREPARE FOR THE FAA TEST — It is important to realize that to become a safe, competent pilot, you need more than just the academic knowledge required to pass a test. For a comprehensive ground training program, we recommend a structured ground school with a qualified flight or ground instructor. An organized course of instruction will help you complete the course in a timely manner, and you will be able to have your questions answered. The additional instruction will be beneficial in your flight training. The sooner you take the test after you complete your study, the better. This way, the information will be fresh in your mind, and you will be more confident when you actually take the FAA computerized test.

WHO CAN TAKE THE TEST — When you are ready to take the FAA computerized test, you must present evidence that you have completed the appropriate ground instruction or a home study course. This proof may be in the form of a graduation certificate from a pilot training course, a written statement, or a logbook entry by a certified ground or flight instructor. Although you are encouraged to obtain ground instruction, a home study course may be used. If you cannot provide one of the above documents, you may present evidence of a completed home study course to an FAA aviation safety inspector for approval.

You also must provide evidence of a permanent mailing address, appropriate identification, and proof of your age. The identification must include a current photograph, your signature, and your residential address, if different from your mailing address. You may present this information in more than one form of identification, such as a driver's license, government identification card, passport, alien residency (green) card, or a military identification card.

FAA COMPUTERIZED TESTS — Detailed information on FAA computer testing is contained in FAA Order 8080.6, Conduct of Airman Knowledge Tests Via The Computer Medium. This FAA order provides guidance for Flight Standards District Offices (FSDOs) and personnel associated with organizations that are participating in, or are seeking to participate in, the FAA Computer-Assisted Airman Knowledge Testing Program. You also may refer to FAA Order 8700.1, General Aviation Operations Inspector's Handbook, for guidance on computer testing by FAR Part 141 pilot schools that hold examining authority.

As a test applicant, you don't need all of the details contained in FAA Orders, but you will be interested in some of the general information about computer testing facilities. A Computer Testing Designee (CTD) is an organization authorized by the FAA to administer FAA airman knowledge tests via the computer medium. A Computer Testing Manager (CTM) is a person selected by the CTD to serve as manager of its national computer testing program. A Testing Center Supervisor (TCS) is a person selected by the CTM, with FAA approval, to administer FAA airman knowledge tests at approved testing centers. The TCS is responsible for the operation of the testing center. A Special Test Administrator (STA) is a person selected by a CTD to administer FAA airman knowledge tests in unique situations and remote or isolated areas. A test proctor is a properly trained and qualified person, appointed by a TCS, authorized to administer FAA airman knowledge tests.

CTDs are selected by the FAA's Flight Standards Service. Those selected may include companies, schools, universities, or other organizations that meet specific requirements. For example, they must clearly demonstrate competence in computer technology, centralized database management, national communications network operation and maintenance, national facilities management, software maintenance and support, and technical training and customer support. They must provide computer-assisted testing, test administration, and data transfer service on a national scale. This means they must maintain a minimum of 20 operational testing centers geographically dispersed throughout the United States. In addition, CTDs must offer operational hours that are convenient to the public. An acceptable plan for test security is also required.

TEST MATERIALS, REFERENCE MATERIALS, AND AIDS — You are allowed to use test materials, reference materials, and aids within specified guidelines, provided the actual test questions or answers are not revealed. All models of aviation-oriented computers, regardless of manufacturer, may be used, including hand-held computers designed expressly for aviation use, and also small electronic calculators that perform arithmetic functions. Simple programmable memories, which allow addition to, subtraction from, or retrieval of one number from the memory, are acceptable. Simple functions such as square root or percent keys are also acceptable.

In addition, you may use any reference materials provided with the test. You will find that these reference materials are the same as those in the Jeppesen Computerized Testing Supplement. They include the legend data and the applicable figures. You also may use scales, straight-edges, protractors, plotters, navigation computers, log sheets, and, as already mentioned, electronic or mechanical calculators that are directly related to the test. Permanently inscribed manufacturer's instructions on the front and back of these aids, such as formulas, conversions, regulations, signals, weather data, holding pattern diagrams, frequencies, weight and balance formulas, and ATC procedures, are permissible.

WHAT TO EXPECT ON A COMPUTERIZED TEST — Computer testing centers are required to have an acceptable method for the "on-line" registration of test applicants during normal business hours. They must provide a dual method for answering questions, such as keyboard, touch screen, or mouse. Features that must be provided also include an introductory lesson to familiarize you with computer testing procedures, the ability to return to a test question previously answered (for the purpose of review or answer changes), and a suitable display of multiple-choice and other question types on the computer screen in one frame. Other required features include a display of the time remaining for the completion of the test, a "HELP" function which permits you to review test questions and optional responses, and provisions for your test score on an Airman Computer Test Report.

On the computerized tests, the selection of questions is done for you, and you will answer the questions that appear on the screen. You will be given a specific amount of time to complete the test, which is based on past experience with others who have taken the exam. If you are prepared, you should have plenty of time to complete the test. After you begin the test, the screen will show you the time remaining for completion. When taking the test, keep the following points in mind:

1. Answer each question in accordance with the latest regulations and procedures. If the regulation or procedure has recently changed, you will receive credit for the affected question. However, these questions will normally be deleted or updated on the FAA computerized tests.
2. Read each question carefully before looking at the possible answers. You should clearly understand the problem before attempting to solve it.
3. After formulating an answer, determine which of the alternatives most nearly corresponds with that answer. The answer chosen should completely resolve the problem.

4. From the answers given, it may appear that there is more than one possible answer; however, there is only one answer that is correct and complete. The other answers are either incomplete or are derived from popular misconceptions.

5. Make sure you select an answer for each question. Questions left unanswered will be counted as incorrect.

6. If a certain question is difficult for you, it is best to proceed to other questions. After you answer the less difficult questions, return to those which were unanswered. The computerized test format helps you identify unanswered questions, as well as those questions you wish to review.

7. When solving a calculator problem, select the answer nearest your solution. The problem has been checked with various types of calculators; therefore, if you have solved it correctly, your answer will be closer to the correct answer than the other choices.

8. Generally, the test results will be available almost immediately. Your score will be recorded on an Airman Computer Test Report form, which includes learning statement codes for incorrect answers. To determine the knowledge area in which a particular question was incorrectly answered, compare the learning statement codes on this report to those in Appendix A in this Question Bank.

Computer testing designees must provide a way for applicants, who challenge the validity of test questions, to enter comments into the computer. In addition to comments, you will be asked to respond to a critique form which may vary at different computer testing centers. The TCS must provide a method for you to respond to critique questions projected on the computer screen. The test proctor should advise you, if you have complaints about test scores, or specific test questions, to write directly to the appropriate FAA office.

RETESTING AFTER FAILURE — The applicant shall surrender the previous test report to the test proctor prior to retesting. The original test report shall be destroyed by the test proctor after administering the retest. The latest test taken will reflect the official score.

As stated in 14 CFR section 61.49, an applicant may apply for retesting after receiving additional training and an endorsement from an authorized instructor who has determined the applicant has been found competent to pass the test.

WHERE TO TAKE THE FAA TEST — Testing is administered via computer at FAA-designated test centers. As indicated, these CTDs are located throughout the U.S. You can expect to pay a fee and the cost varies at different locations. The following is a listing of the approved computer testing designees at the time of publication of this question bank. You may want to check with your local FSDO for changes.

Computer Assisted Testing Service (CATS)
1-800-947-4228
Outside U.S. (650) 259-8550

PSI/LaserGrade Computer Testing
1-800-211-2754
Outside U.S. (360) 896-9111

General Instructions

Your instructor can advise you on the best way to utilize this question bank. This question bank also includes a complete answer key, question selection sheets, and exam answer forms. Final exams are drawn from the question bank by way of the question selection sheets. Mark the answer you select for each question on the exam answer form. Answers for all FAA questions are also provided on the answer key. The FAA minimum passing grade is 70.

Private Pilot Airman Knowledge Test Question Bank

1. PLT371
With respect to the certification of airmen, which is a category of aircraft?

A — Gyroplane, helicopter, airship, free balloon.
B — Airplane, rotorcraft, glider, lighter-than-air.
C — Single-engine land and sea, multiengine land and sea.

2. PLT371
With respect to the certification of airmen, which is a class of aircraft?

A — Airplane, rotorcraft, glider, lighter-than-air.
B — Single-engine land and sea, multiengine land and sea.
C — Lighter-than-air, airship, hot air balloon, gas balloon.

3. PLT371
With respect to the certification of aircraft, which is a category of aircraft?

A — Normal, utility, acrobatic.
B — Airplane, rotorcraft, glider.
C — Landplane, seaplane.

4. PLT371
With respect to the certification of aircraft, which is a class of aircraft?

A — Normal, utility, acrobatic, limited.
B — Airplane, rotorcraft, glider, balloon.
C — Transport, restricted, provisional.

5. PLT463
How soon after the conviction for driving while intoxicated by alcohol or drugs shall it be reported to the FAA, Civil Aviation Security Division?

A — No later than 60 days after the motor vehicle action.
B — No later than 30 working days after the motor vehicle action.
C — Required to be reported upon renewal of medical certificate.

6. PLT373
Where may an aircraft's operating limitations be found?

A — On the Airworthiness Certificate.
B — In the current, FAA-approved flight manual, approved manual material, markings, and placards, or any combination thereof.
C — In the aircraft airframe and engine logbooks.

7. PLT170
To minimize the side loads placed on the landing gear during touchdown, the pilot should keep the

A — direction of motion of the aircraft parallel to the runway.
B — longitudinal axis of the aircraft parallel to the direction of its motion.
C — downwind wing lowered sufficiently to eliminate the tendency for the aircraft to drift.

8. PLT377
Where may an aircraft's operating limitations be found if the aircraft has an Experimental or Special light-sport airworthiness certificate?

A — Attached to the Airworthiness Certificate.
B — In the current, FAA-approved flight manual.
C — In the aircraft airframe and engine logbooks.

9. PLT342
Excessively high engine temperatures will

A — cause damage to heat-conducting hoses and warping of the cylinder cooling fins.
B — cause loss of power, excessive oil consumption, and possible permanent internal engine damage.
C — not appreciably affect an aircraft engine.

10. PLT342

If the engine oil temperature and cylinder head temperature gauges have exceeded their normal operating range, the pilot may have been operating with

A — the mixture set too rich.
B — higher-than-normal oil pressure.
C — too much power and with the mixture set too lean.

11. PLT478

One purpose of the dual ignition system on an aircraft engine is to provide for

A — improved engine performance.
B — uniform heat distribution.
C — balanced cylinder head pressure.

12. PLT253

On aircraft equipped with fuel pumps, when is the auxiliary electric driven pump used?

A — In the event engine-driven fuel pump fails.
B — All the time to aid the engine-driven fuel pump.
C — Constantly except in starting the engine.

13. PLT191

The operating principle of float-type carburetors is based on the

A — automatic metering of air at the venturi as the aircraft gains altitude.
B — difference in air pressure at the venturi throat and the air inlet.
C — increase in air velocity in the throat of a venturi causing an increase in air pressure.

14. PLT191

The basic purpose of adjusting the fuel/air mixture at altitude is to

A — decrease the amount of fuel in the mixture in order to compensate for increased air density.
B — decrease the fuel flow in order to compensate for decreased air density.
C — increase the amount of fuel in the mixture to compensate for the decrease in pressure and density of the air.

15. PLT249

During the run-up at a high-elevation airport, a pilot notes a slight engine roughness that is not affected by the magneto check but grows worse during the carburetor heat check. Under these circumstances, what would be the most logical initial action?

A — Check the results obtained with a leaner setting of the mixture.
B — Taxi back to the flight line for a maintenance check.
C — Reduce manifold pressure to control detonation.

16. PLT249

While cruising at 9,500 feet MSL, the fuel/air mixture is properly adjusted. What will occur if a descent to 4,500 feet MSL is made without readjusting the mixture?

A — The fuel/air mixture may become excessively lean.
B — There will be more fuel in the cylinders than is needed for normal combustion, and the excess fuel will absorb heat and cool the engine.
C — The excessively rich mixture will create higher cylinder head temperatures and may cause detonation.

17. PLT190

Which condition is most favorable to the development of carburetor icing?

A — Any temperature below freezing and a relative humidity of less than 50 percent.
B — Temperature between 32° and 50°F and low humidity.
C — Temperature between 20° and 70°F and high humidity.

18. PLT190

The possibility of carburetor icing exists even when the ambient air temperature is as

A — high as 70°F and the relative humidity is high.
B — high as 95°F and there is visible moisture.
C — low as 0°F and the relative humidity is high.

19. PLT190
If an aircraft is equipped with a fixed-pitch propeller and a float-type carburetor, the first indication of carburetor ice would most likely be

A — a drop in oil temperature and cylinder head temperature.
B — engine roughness.
C — loss of RPM.

20. PLT189
Applying carburetor heat will

A — result in more air going through the carburetor.
B — enrich the fuel/air mixture.
C — not affect the fuel/air mixture.

21. PLT189
What change occurs in the fuel/air mixture when carburetor heat is applied?

A — A decrease in RPM results from the lean mixture.
B — The fuel/air mixture becomes richer.
C — The fuel/air mixture becomes leaner.

22. PLT189
Generally speaking, the use of carburetor heat tends to

A — decrease engine performance.
B — increase engine performance.
C — have no effect on engine performance.

23. PLT189
The presence of carburetor ice in an aircraft equipped with a fixed-pitch propeller can be verified by applying carburetor heat and noting

A — an increase in RPM and then a gradual decrease in RPM.
B — a decrease in RPM and then a constant RPM indication.
C — a decrease in RPM and then a gradual increase in RPM.

24. PLT191
With regard to carburetor ice, float-type carburetor systems in comparison to fuel injection systems are generally considered to be

A — more susceptible to icing.
B — equally susceptible to icing.
C — susceptible to icing only when visible moisture is present.

25. PLT250
If the grade of fuel used in an aircraft engine is lower than specified for the engine, it will most likely cause

A — a mixture of fuel and air that is not uniform in all cylinders.
B — lower cylinder head temperatures.
C — detonation.

26. PLT115
Detonation occurs in a reciprocating aircraft engine when

A — the spark plugs are fouled or shorted out or the wiring is defective.
B — hot spots in the combustion chamber ignite the fuel/air mixture in advance of normal ignition.
C — the unburned charge in the cylinders explodes instead of burning normally.

27. PLT115
Detonation may occur at high-power settings when

A — the fuel mixture ignites instantaneously instead of burning progressively and evenly.
B — an excessively rich fuel mixture causes an explosive gain in power.
C — the fuel mixture is ignited too early by hot carbon deposits in the cylinder.

28. PLT115
If a pilot suspects that the engine (with a fixed-pitch propeller) is detonating during climb-out after takeoff, the initial corrective action to take would be to

A — lean the mixture.
B — lower the nose slightly to increase airspeed.
C — apply carburetor heat.

29. PLT249
The uncontrolled firing of the fuel/air charge in advance of normal spark ignition is known as

A — combustion.
B — pre-ignition.
C — detonation.

30. PLT250
Which would most likely cause the cylinder head temperature and engine oil temperature gauges to exceed their normal operating ranges?

A — Using fuel that has a lower-than-specified fuel rating.
B — Using fuel that has a higher-than-specified fuel rating.
C — Operating with higher-than-normal oil pressure.

31. PLT250
What type fuel can be substituted for an aircraft if the recommended octane is not available?

A — The next higher octane aviation gas.
B — The next lower octane aviation gas.
C — Unleaded automotive gas of the same octane rating.

32. PLT250
Filling the fuel tanks after the last flight of the day is considered a good operating procedure because this will

A — force any existing water to the top of the tank away from the fuel lines to the engine.
B — prevent expansion of the fuel by eliminating airspace in the tanks.
C — prevent moisture condensation by eliminating airspace in the tanks.

33. PLT324
For internal cooling, reciprocating aircraft engines are especially dependent on

A — a properly functioning thermostat.
B — air flowing over the exhaust manifold.
C — the circulation of lubricating oil.

34. PLT324
An abnormally high engine oil temperature indication may be caused by

A — the oil level being too low.
B — operating with a too high viscosity oil.
C — operating with an excessively rich mixture.

35. PLT342
What action can a pilot take to aid in cooling an engine that is overheating during a climb?

A — Reduce rate of climb and increase airspeed.
B — Reduce climb speed and increase RPM.
C — Increase climb speed and increase RPM.

36. PLT342
What is one procedure to aid in cooling an engine that is overheating?

A — Enrich the fuel mixture.
B — Increase the RPM.
C — Reduce the airspeed.

37. PLT342
How is engine operation controlled on an engine equipped with a constant-speed propeller?

A — The throttle controls power output as registered on the manifold pressure gauge and the propeller control regulates engine RPM.
B — The throttle controls power output as registered on the manifold pressure gauge and the propeller control regulates a constant blade angle.
C — The throttle controls engine RPM as registered on the tachometer and the mixture control regulates the power output.

38. PLT350
What is an advantage of a constant-speed propeller?

A — Permits the pilot to select and maintain a desired cruising speed.
B — Permits the pilot to select the blade angle for the most efficient performance.
C — Provides a smoother operation with stable RPM and eliminates vibrations.

39. PLT351
A precaution for the operation of an engine equipped with a constant-speed propeller is to

A — avoid high RPM settings with high manifold pressure.
B — avoid high manifold pressure settings with low RPM.
C — always use a rich mixture with high RPM settings.

40. PLT479
What should be the first action after starting an aircraft engine?

A — Adjust for proper RPM and check for desired indications on the engine gauges.
B — Place the magneto or ignition switch momentarily in the OFF position to check for proper grounding.
C — Test each brake and the parking brake.

41. PLT479
Should it become necessary to handprop an airplane engine, it is extremely important that a competent pilot

A — call "contact" before touching the propeller.
B — be at the controls in the cockpit.
C — be in the cockpit and call out all commands.

42. PLT342
Excessively high engine temperatures, either in the air or on the ground, will

A — increase fuel consumption and may increase power due to the increased heat.
B — result in damage to heat-conducting hoses and warping of cylinder cooling fans.
C — cause loss of power, excessive oil consumption, and possible permanent internal engine damage.

43. PLT254
To properly purge water from the fuel system of an aircraft equipped with fuel tank sumps and a fuel strainer quick drain, it is necessary to drain fuel from the

A — fuel strainer drain.
B — lowest point in the fuel system.
C — fuel strainer drain and the fuel tank sumps.

44. PLT506
Which V-speed represents maneuvering speed?

A — V_A
B — V_{LO}
C — V_{NE}

45. PLT166
If an altimeter setting is not available before flight, to which altitude should the pilot adjust the altimeter?

A — The elevation of the nearest airport corrected to mean sea level.
B — The elevation of the departure area.
C — Pressure altitude corrected for nonstandard temperature.

46. PLT166
Prior to takeoff, the altimeter should be set to which altitude or altimeter setting?

A — The current local altimeter setting, if available, or the departure airport elevation.
B — The corrected density altitude of the departure airport.
C — The corrected pressure altitude for the departure airport.

47. PLT337
If the pitot tube and outside static vents become clogged, which instruments would be affected?

A — The altimeter, airspeed indicator, and turn-and-slip indicator.
B — The altimeter, airspeed indicator, and vertical speed indicator.
C — The altimeter, attitude indicator, and turn-and-slip indicator.

48. PLT337
Which instrument will become inoperative if the pitot tube becomes clogged?

A — Altimeter.
B — Vertical speed.
C — Airspeed.

49. PLT337
Which instrument(s) will become inoperative if the static vents become clogged?

A — Airspeed only.
B — Altimeter only.
C — Airspeed, altimeter, and vertical speed.

50. PLT041
(Refer to figure 3)
Altimeter 1 indicates

A — 500 feet.
B — 1,500 feet.
C — 10,500 feet.

51. PLT041
(Refer to figure 3)
Altimeter 2 indicates

A — 1,500 feet.
B — 4,500 feet.
C — 14,500 feet.

52. PLT041
(Refer to figure 3)
Altimeter 3 indicates

A — 9,500 feet.
B — 10,950 feet.
C — 15,940 feet.

53. PLT041
(Refer to figure 3)
Which altimeter(s) indicate(s) more than 10,000 feet?

A — 1, 2, and 3
B — 1 and 2 only
C — 1 only

54. PLT166
Altimeter setting is the value to which the barometric pressure scale of the altimeter is set so the altimeter indicates

A — calibrated altitude at field elevation.
B — absolute altitude at field elevation.
C — true altitude at field elevation.

55. PLT165
How do variations in temperature affect the altimeter?

A — Pressure levels are raised on warm days and the indicated altitude is lower than true altitude.
B — Higher temperatures expand the pressure levels and the indicated altitude is higher than true altitude.
C — Lower temperatures lower the pressure levels and the indicated altitude is lower than true altitude.

56. PLT023
What is true altitude?

A — The vertical distance of the aircraft above sea level.
B — The vertical distance of the aircraft above the surface.
C — The height above the standard datum plane.

57. PLT023
What is absolute altitude?

A — The altitude read directly from the altimeter.
B — The vertical distance of the aircraft above the surface.
C — The height above the standard datum plane.

58. PLT023
What is density altitude?

A — The height above the standard datum plane.
B — The pressure altitude corrected for nonstandard temperature.
C — The altitude read directly from the altimeter.

59. PLT023
What is pressure altitude?

A — The indicated altitude corrected for position and installation error.
B — The altitude indicated when the barometric pressure scale is set to 29.92.
C — The indicated altitude corrected for nonstandard temperature and pressure.

60. PLT023
Under what condition is indicated altitude the same as true altitude?

A — If the altimeter has no mechanical error.
B — When at sea level under standard conditions.
C — When at 18,000 feet MSL with the altimeter set at 29.92.

61. PLT167
If it is necessary to set the altimeter from 29.15 to 29.85, what change occurs?

A — 70-foot increase in indicated altitude.
B — 70-foot increase in density altitude.
C — 700-foot increase in indicated altitude.

62. PLT337
The pitot system provides impact pressure for which instrument?

A — Altimeter.
B — Vertical-speed indicator.
C — Airspeed indicator.

63. PLT123
As altitude increases, the indicated airspeed at which a given airplane stalls in a particular configuration will

A — decrease as the true airspeed decreases.
B — decrease as the true airspeed increases.
C — remain the same regardless of altitude.

64. PLT088
What does the red line on an airspeed indicator represent?

A — Maneuvering speed.
B — Turbulent or rough-air speed.
C — Never-exceed speed.

65. PLT088
(Refer to figure 4)
What is the full flap operating range for the airplane?

A — 60 to 100 MPH.
B — 60 to 208 MPH.
C — 65 to 165 MPH.

66. PLT088
(Refer to figure 4)
What is the caution range of the airplane?

A — 0 to 60 MPH.
B — 100 to 165 MPH.
C — 165 to 208 MPH.

67. PLT088
(Refer to figure 4)
The maximum speed at which the airplane can be operated in smooth air is

A — 100 MPH.
B — 165 MPH.
C — 208 MPH.

68. PLT088
(Refer to figure 4)
Which color identifies the never-exceed speed?

A — Lower limit of the yellow arc.
B — Upper limit of the white arc.
C — The red radial line.

69. PLT088
(Refer to figure 4)
Which color identifies the power-off stalling speed in a specified configuration?

A — Upper limit of the green arc.
B — Upper limit of the white arc.
C — Lower limit of the green arc.

70. PLT088
(Refer to figure 4)
What is the maximum flaps-extended speed?

A — 65 MPH.
B — 100 MPH.
C — 165 MPH.

71. PLT088
(Refer to figure 4)
Which color identifies the normal flap operating range?

A — The lower limit of the white arc to the upper limit of the green arc.
B — The green arc.
C — The white arc.

72. PLT088
(Refer to figure 4)
Which color identifies the power-off stalling speed with wing flaps and landing gear in the landing configuration?

A — Upper limit of the green arc.
B — Upper limit of the white arc.
C — Lower limit of the white arc.

73. PLT088
(Refer to figure 4)
What is the maximum structural cruising speed?

A — 100 MPH.
B — 165 MPH.
C — 208 MPH.

74. PLT088
What is an important airspeed limitation that is not color coded on airspeed indicators?

A — Never-exceed speed.
B — Maximum structural cruising speed.
C — Maneuvering speed.

75. PLT086
(Refer to figure 5)
A turn coordinator provides an indication of the

A — movement of the aircraft about the yaw and roll axis.
B — angle of bank up to but not exceeding 30°.
C — attitude of the aircraft with reference to the longitudinal axis.

76. PLT278
(Refer to figure 7)
The proper adjustment to make on the attitude indicator during level flight is to align the

A — horizon bar to the level-flight indication.
B — horizon bar to the miniature airplane.
C — miniature airplane to the horizon bar.

77. PLT278
(Refer to figure 7)
How should a pilot determine the direction of bank from an attitude indicator such as the one illustrated?

A — By the direction of deflection of the banking scale (A).
B — By the direction of deflection of the horizon bar (B).
C — By the relationship of the miniature airplane (C) to the deflected horizon bar (B).

78. PLT215
Deviation in a magnetic compass is caused by the

A — presence of flaws in the permanent magnets of the compass.
B — difference in the location between true north and magnetic north.
C — magnetic fields within the aircraft distorting the lines of magnetic force.

79. PLT215
In the Northern Hemisphere, a magnetic compass will normally indicate initially a turn toward the west if

A — a left turn is entered from a north heading.
B — a right turn is entered from a north heading.
C — an aircraft is accelerated while on a north heading.

80. PLT215
In the Northern Hemisphere, a magnetic compass will normally indicate initially a turn toward the east if

A — an aircraft is decelerated while on a south heading.
B — an aircraft is accelerated while on a north heading.
C — a left turn is entered from a north heading.

81. PLT215
In the Northern Hemisphere, a magnetic compass will normally indicate a turn toward the north if

A — a left turn is entered from an westheading.
B — an aircraft is decelerated while on an east or west heading.
C — an aircraft is accelerated while on an east or west heading.

82. PLT215
In the Northern Hemisphere, the magnetic compass will normally indicate a turn toward the south when

A — a left turn is entered from an east heading.
B — a right turn is entered from a west heading.
C — the aircraft is decelerated while on a west heading.

83. PLT215
In the Northern Hemisphere, if an aircraft is accelerated or decelerated, the magnetic compass will normally indicate

A — a turn momentarily.
B — correctly when on a north or south heading.
C — a turn toward the south.

84. PLT215
During flight, when are the indications of a magnetic compass accurate?

A — Only in straight-and-level unaccelerated flight.
B — As long as the airspeed is constant.
C — During turns if the bank does not exceed 18°.

85. PLT206
If the outside air temperature (OAT) at a given altitude is warmer than standard, the density altitude is

A — equal to pressure altitude.
B — lower than pressure altitude.
C — higher than pressure altitude.

86. PLT173
What are the standard temperature and pressure values for sea level?

A — 15°C and 29.92 inches Hg.
B — 59°C and 1013.2 millibars.
C — 59°F and 29.92 millibars.

87. PLT173
If a pilot changes the altimeter setting from 30.11 to 29.96, what is the approximate change in indication?

A — Altimeter will indicate .15 inches Hg higher.
B — Altimeter will indicate 150 feet higher.
C — Altimeter will indicate 150 feet lower.

88. PLT023
Under which condition will pressure altitude be equal to true altitude?

A — When the atmospheric pressure is 29.92 inches Hg.
B — When standard atmospheric conditions exist.
C — When indicated altitude is equal to the pressure altitude.

89. PLT023
Under what condition is pressure altitude and density altitude the same value?

A — At sea level, when the temperature is 0°F.
B — When the altimeter has no installation error.
C — At standard temperature.

90. PLT041
If a flight is made from an area of low pressure into an area of high pressure without the altimeter setting being adjusted, the altimeter will indicate

A — the actual altitude above sea level.
B — higher than the actual altitude above sea level.
C — lower than the actual altitude above sea level.

91. PLT041
If a flight is made from an area of high pressure into an area of lower pressure without the altimeter setting being adjusted, the altimeter will indicate

A — lower than the actual altitude above sea level.
B — higher than the actual altitude above sea level.
C — the actual altitude above sea level.

92. PLT165
Under what condition will true altitude be lower than indicated altitude?

A — In colder than standard air temperature.
B — In warmer than standard air temperature.
C — When density altitude is higher than indicated altitude.

93. PLT165
Which condition would cause the altimeter to indicate a lower altitude than true altitude?

A — Air temperature lower than standard.
B — Atmospheric pressure lower than standard.
C — Air temperature warmer than standard.

94. PLT023
Which factor would tend to increase the density altitude at a given airport?

A — An increase in barometric pressure.
B — An increase in ambient temperature.
C — A decrease in relative humidity.

95. PLT215
The angular difference between true north and magnetic north is

A — magnetic deviation.
B — magnetic variation.
C — compass acceleration error.

96. PLT215
In the Northern Hemisphere, a magnetic compass will normally indicate a turn toward the north if

A — a left turn is entered from a west heading.
B — an aircraft is decelerated while on an east or west heading.
C — an aircraft is accelerated while on an east or west heading.

97. PLT215
What should be the indication on the magnetic compass as you roll into a standard rate turn to the right from a south heading in the Northern Hemisphere?

A — The compass will initially indicate a turn to the left.
B — The compass will indicate a turn to the right, but at a faster rate than is actually occurring.
C — The compass will remain on south for a short time, then gradually catch up to the magnetic heading of the airplane.

98. PLT215
When converting from true course to magnetic heading, a pilot should

A — subtract easterly variation and right wind correction angle.
B — add westerly variation and subtract left wind correction angle.
C — subtract westerly variation and add right wind correction angle.

99. PLT247
The four forces acting on an airplane in flight are

A — lift, weight, thrust, and drag.
B — lift, weight, gravity, and thrust.
C — lift, gravity, power, and friction.

100. PLT247
When are the four forces that act on an airplane in equilibrium?

A — During unaccelerated flight.
B — When the aircraft is accelerating.
C — When the aircraft is at rest on the ground.

101. PLT168
(Refer to figure 1)
The acute angle A is the angle of

A — incidence.
B — attack.
C — dihedral.

102. PLT168
The term "angle of attack" is defined as the angle

A — between the wing chord line and the relative wind.
B — between the airplane's climb angle and the horizon.
C — formed by the longitudinal axis of the airplane and the chord line of the wing.

103. PLT247
What is the relationship of lift, drag, thrust, and weight when the airplane is in straight-and-level flight?

A — Lift equals weight and thrust equals drag.
B — Lift, drag, and weight equal thrust.
C — Lift and weight equal thrust and drag.

104. PLT473
One of the main functions of flaps during approach and landing is to

A — decrease the angle of descent without increasing the airspeed.
B — permit a touchdown at a higher indicated airspeed.
C — increase the angle of descent without increasing the airspeed.

105. PLT473
What is one purpose of wing flaps?

A — To enable the pilot to make steeper approaches to a landing without increasing the airspeed.
B — To relieve the pilot of maintaining continuous pressure on the controls.
C — To decrease wing area to vary the lift.

106. PLT168
The angle of attack at which an airplane wing stalls will

A — increase if the CG is moved forward.
B — change with an increase in gross weight.
C — remain the same regardless of gross weight.

107. PLT131
What is ground effect?

A — The result of the interference of the surface of the Earth with the airflow patterns about an airplane.
B — The result of an alteration in airflow patterns increasing induced drag about the wings of an airplane.
C — The result of the disruption of the airflow patterns about the wings of an airplane to the point where the wings will no longer support the airplane in flight.

108. PLT131
Floating caused by the phenomenon of ground effect will be most realized during an approach to land when at

A — less than the length of the wingspan above the surface.
B — twice the length of the wingspan above the surface.
C — a higher-than-normal angle of attack.

109. PLT131
What must a pilot be aware of as a result of ground effect?

A — Wingtip vortices increase creating wake turbulence problems for arriving and departing aircraft.
B — Induced drag decreases; therefore, any excess speed at the point of flare may cause considerable floating.
C — A full stall landing will require less up elevator deflection than would a full stall when done free of ground effect.

110. PLT131
Ground effect is most likely to result in which problem?

A — Setting to the surface abruptly during landing.
B — Becoming airborne before reaching recommended takeoff speed.
C — Inability to get airborne even though airspeed is sufficient for normal takeoff needs.

111. PLT025
Which statement relates to Bernoulli's principle?

A — For every action there is an equal and opposite reaction.
B — An additional upward force is generated as the lower surface of the wing deflects air downward.
C — Air traveling faster over the curved upper surface of an airfoil causes lower pressure on the top surface.

112. PLT168
The angle between the chord line of an airfoil and the relative wind is known as the angle of

A — lift.
B — attack.
C — incidence.

113. PLT236
Changes in the center of pressure of a wing affect the aircraft's

A — lift/drag ratio.
B — lifting capacity.
C — aerodynamic balance and controllability.

114. PLT213
An airplane said to be inherently stable will

A — be difficult to stall.
B — require less effort to control.
C — not spin.

115. PLT213
What determines the longitudinal stability of an airplane?

A — The location of the CG with respect to the center of lift.
B — The effectiveness of the horizontal stabilizer, rudder, and rudder trim tab.
C — The relationship of thrust and lift to weight and drag.

116. PLT351
What causes an airplane (except a T-tail) to pitch nosedown when power is reduced and controls are not adjusted?

A — The CG shifts forward when thrust and drag are reduced.
B — The downwash on the elevators from the propeller slipstream is reduced and elevator effectiveness is reduced.
C — When thrust is reduced to less than weight, lift is also reduced and the wings can no longer support the weight.

117. PLT240
An airplane has been loaded in such a manner that the CG is located aft of the aft CG limit. One undesirable flight characteristic a pilot might experience with this airplane would be

A — a longer takeoff run.
B — difficulty in recovering from a stalled condition.
C — stalling at higher-than-normal airspeed.

118. PLT240
Loading an airplane to the most aft CG will cause the airplane to be

A — less stable at all speeds.
B — less stable at slow speeds, but more stable at high speeds.
C — less stable at high speeds, but more stable at low speeds.

119. PLT245
In what flight condition must an aircraft be placed in order to spin?

A — Partially stalled with one wing low.
B — In a steep diving spiral.
C — Stalled.

120. PLT245
During a spin to the left, which wing(s) is/are stalled?

A — Both wings are stalled.
B — Neither wing is stalled.
C — Only the left wing is stalled.

121. PLT243
In what flight condition is torque effect the greatest in a single-engine airplane?

A — Low airspeed, high power, high angle of attack.
B — Low airspeed, low power, low angle of attack.
C — High airspeed, high power, high angle of attack.

122. PLT243
The left turning tendency of an airplane caused by P-factor is the result of the

A — clockwise rotation of the engine and the propeller turning the airplane counter-clockwise.
B — propeller blade descending on the right, producing more thrust than the ascending blade on the left.
C — gyroscopic forces applied to the rotating propeller blades acting 90° in advance of the point the force was applied.

123. PLT243
When does P-factor cause the airplane to yaw to the left?

A — When at low angles of attack.
B — When at high angles of attack.
C — When at high airspeeds.

124. PLT309
(Refer to figure 2)
If an airplane weighs 2,300 pounds, what approximate weight would the airplane structure be required to support during a 60° banked turn while maintaining altitude?

A — 2,300 pounds.
B — 3,400 pounds.
C — 4,600 pounds.

125. PLT309
(Refer to figure 2)
If an airplane weighs 3,300 pounds, what approximate weight would the airplane structure be required to support during a 30° banked turn while maintaining altitude?

A — 1,200 pounds.
B — 3,100 pounds.
C — 3,960 pounds.

126. PLT309
(Refer to figure 2)
If an airplane weighs 4,500 pounds, what approximate weight would the airplane structure be required to support during a 45° banked turn while maintaining altitude?

A — 4,500 pounds.
B — 6,750 pounds.
C — 7,200 pounds.

127. PLT311
The amount of excess load that can be imposed on the wing of an airplane depends upon the

A — position of the CG.
B — speed of the airplane.
C — abruptness at which the load is applied.

128. PLT310
Which basic flight maneuver increases the load factor on an airplane as compared to straight-and-level flight?

A — Climbs.
B — Turns.
C — Stalls.

129. PLT242
What force makes an airplane turn?

A — The horizontal component of lift.
B — The vertical component of lift.
C — Centrifugal force.

130. PLT018
During an approach to a stall, an increased load factor will cause the airplane to

A — stall at a higher airspeed.
B — have a tendency to spin.
C — be more difficult to control.

131. PLT219
Select the four flight fundamentals involved in maneuvering an aircraft.

A — Aircraft power, pitch, bank, and trim.
B — Starting, taxiing, takeoff, and landing.
C — Straight-and-level flight, turns, climbs, and descents.

132. PLT414
Which aircraft has the right-of-way over all other air traffic?

A — A balloon.
B — An aircraft in distress.
C — An aircraft on final approach to land.

133. PLT414
What action is required when two aircraft of the same category converge, but not head-on?

A — The faster aircraft shall give way.
B — The aircraft on the left shall give way.
C — Each aircraft shall give way to the right.

134. PLT414
Which aircraft has the right-of-way over the other aircraft listed?

A — Glider.
B — Airship.
C — Aircraft refueling other aircraft.

135. PLT414
An airplane and an airship are converging. If the airship is left of the airplane's position, which aircraft has the right-of-way?

A — The airship.
B — The airplane.
C — Each pilot should alter course to the right.

136. PLT414
Which aircraft has the right-of-way over the other aircraft listed?

A — Airship.
B — Aircraft towing other aircraft.
C — Gyroplane.

137. PLT414
What action should the pilots of a glider and an airplane take if on a head-on collision course?

A — The airplane pilot should give way to the left.
B — The glider pilot should give way to the right.
C — Both pilots should give way to the right.

138. PLT414
When two or more aircraft are approaching an airport for the purpose of landing, the right-of-way belongs to the aircraft

A — that has the other to its right.
B — that is the least maneuverable.
C — at the lower altitude, but it shall not take advantage of this rule to cut in front of or to overtake another.

139. PLT430
Except when necessary for takeoff or landing, what is the minimum safe altitude for a pilot to operate an aircraft anywhere?

A — An altitude allowing, if a power unit fails, an emergency landing without undue hazard to persons or property on the surface.
B — An altitude of 500 feet above the surface and no closer than 500 feet to any person, vessel, vehicle, or structure.
C — An altitude of 500 feet above the highest obstacle within a horizontal radius of 1,000 feet.

140. PLT430
Except when necessary for takeoff or landing, what is the minimum safe altitude required for a pilot to operate an aircraft over congested areas?

A — An altitude of 1,000 feet above any person, vessel, vehicle, or structure.
B — An altitude of 500 feet above the highest obstacle within a horizontal radius of 1,000 feet.
C — An altitude of 1,000 feet above the highest obstacle within a horizontal radius of 2,000 feet.

141. PLT430
Except when necessary for takeoff or landing, what is the minimum safe altitude for a pilot to operate an aircraft over other than a congested area?

A — An altitude allowing, if a power unit fails, an emergency landing without undue hazard to persons or property on the surface.
B — An altitude of 500 feet AGL, except over open water or a sparsely populated area, which requires 500 feet from any person, vessel, vehicle, or structure.
C — An altitude of 500 feet above the highest obstacle within a horizontal radius of 1,000 feet.

142. PLT430
Except when necessary for takeoff or landing, an aircraft may not be operated closer than what distance from any person, vessel, vehicle, or structure?

A — 500 feet.
B — 700 feet.
C — 1,000 feet.

143. PLT485
When taxiing with strong quartering tailwinds, which aileron positions should be used?

A — Aileron down on the downwind side.
B — Ailerons neutral.
C — Aileron down on the side from which the wind is blowing.

144. PLT485
Which aileron positions should a pilot generally use when taxiing in strong quartering headwinds?

A — Aileron up on the side from which the wind is blowing.
B — Aileron down on the side from which the wind is blowing.
C — Ailerons neutral.

145. PLT485
Which wind condition would be most critical when taxiing a nosewheel equipped high-wing airplane?

A — Quartering tailwind.
B — Direct crosswind.
C — Quartering headwind.

146. PLT485
(Refer to figure 9)
(Area A) How should the flight controls be held while taxiing a tricycle-gear equipped airplane into a left quartering headwind?

A — Left aileron up, elevator neutral.
B — Left aileron down, elevator neutral.
C — Left aileron up, elevator down.

147. PLT485
(Refer to figure 9)
(Area B) How should the flight controls be held while taxiing a tailwheel airplane into a right quartering headwind?

A — Right aileron up, elevator up.
B — Right aileron down, elevator neutral.
C — Right aileron up, elevator down.

148. PLT485
(Refer to figure 9)
(Area C) How should the flight controls be held while taxiing a tailwheel airplane with a left quartering tailwind?

A — Left aileron up, elevator neutral.
B — Left aileron down, elevator neutral.
C — Left aileron down, elevator down.

149. PLT194
Prior to starting each maneuver, pilots should

A — check altitude, airspeed, and heading indications.
B — visually scan the entire area for collision avoidance.
C — announce their intentions on the nearest CTAF.

150. PLT125
What procedure is recommended when climbing or descending VFR on an airway?

A — Execute gentle banks, left and right for continuous visual scanning of the airspace.
B — Advise the nearest FSS of the altitude changes.
C — Fly away from the centerline of the airway before changing altitude.

151. PLT194
What effect does haze have on the ability to see traffic or terrain features during flight?

A — Haze causes the eyes to focus at infinity.
B — The eyes tend to overwork in haze and do not detect relative movement easily.
C — All traffic or terrain features appear to be farther away than their actual distance.

152. PLT194
The most effective method of scanning for other aircraft for collision avoidance during daylight hours is to use

A — regularly spaced concentration on the 3-, 9-, and 12-o'clock positions.
B — a series of short, regularly spaced eye movements to search each 10-degree sector.
C — peripheral vision by scanning small sectors and utilizing offcenter viewing.

153. PLT194
Which technique should a pilot use to scan for traffic to the right and left during straight-and-level flight?

A — Systematically focus on different segments of the sky for short intervals.
B — Concentrate on relative movement detected in the peripheral vision area.
C — Continuous sweeping of the windshield from right to left.

154. PLT194
How can you determine if another aircraft is on a collision course with your aircraft?

A — The other aircraft will always appear to get larger and closer at a rapid rate.
B — The nose of each aircraft is pointed at the same point in space.
C — There will be no apparent relative motion between your aircraft and the other aircraft.

155. PLT194
Most midair collision accidents occur during

A — hazy days.
B — clear days.
C — cloudy nights.

156. PLT147
While operating in class D airspace, each pilot of an aircraft approaching to land on a runway served by a visual approach slope indicator (VASI) shall

A — maintain a 3° glide until approximately 1/2 mile to the runway before going below the VASI.
B — maintain an altitude at or above the glide slope until a lower altitude is necessary for a safe landing.
C — stay high until the runway can be reached in a power-off landing.

157. PLT147
When approaching to land on a runway served by a visual approach slope indicator (VASI), the pilot shall

A — maintain an altitude that captures the glide slope at least 2 miles downwind from the runway threshold.
B — maintain an altitude at or above the glide slope.
C — remain on the glide slope and land between the two-light bar.

158. PLT141
Airport taxiway edge lights are identified at night by

A — white directional lights.
B — blue omnidirectional lights.
C — alternate red and green lights.

159. PLT147
A slightly high glide slope indication from a precision approach path indicator is

A — four white lights.
B — three white lights and one red light.
C — two white lights and two red lights.

160. PLT147
A below glide slope indication from a tri-color VASI is a

A — red light signal.
B — pink light signal.
C — green light signal.

161. PLT147
An above glide slope indication from a tri-color VASI is

A — a white light signal.
B — a green light signal.
C — an amber light signal.

162. PLT147
An on glide slope indication from a tri-color VASI is

A — a white light signal.
B — a green light signal.
C — an amber light signal.

163. PLT147
A below glide slope indication from a pulsating approach slope indicator is a

A — pulsating white light.
B — steady white light.
C — pulsating red light.

164. PLT147
(Refer to figure 48)
Illustration A indicates that the aircraft is

A — below the glide slope.
B — on the glide slope.
C — above the glide slope.

165. PLT147
(Refer to figure 48)
VASI lights as shown by illustration C indicate that the airplane is

A — off course to the left.
B — above the glide slope.
C — below the glide slope.

166. PLT147
(Refer to figure 48)
While on final approach to a runway equipped with a standard 2-bar VASI, the lights appear as shown by illustration D. This means that the aircraft is

A — above the glide slope.
B — below the glide slope.
C — on the glide slope.

167. PLT145
To set the high intensity runway lights on medium intensity, the pilot should click the microphone seven times, then click it

A — one time within four seconds.
B — three times within three seconds.
C — five times within five seconds.

168. PLT141
An airport's rotating beacon operated during daylight hours indicates

A — there are obstructions on the airport.
B — that weather at the airport located in Class D airspace is below basic VFR weather minimums.
C — the Airport Traffic Control tower is not in operation.

169. PLT141
A military air station can be identified by a rotating beacon that emits

A — white and green alternating flashes.
B — two quick, white flashes between green flashes.
C — green, yellow, and white flashes.

170. PLT141
How can a military airport be identified at night?

A — Alternate white and green light flashes.
B — Dual peaked (two quick) white flashes between green flashes.
C — White flashing lights with steady green at the same location.

171. PLT141
(Refer to figure 49)
That portion of the runway identified by the letter A may be used for

A — landing.
B — taxiing and takeoff.
C — taxiing and landing.

172. PLT077
(Refer to figure 49)
According to the airport diagram, which statement is true?

A — Runway 30 is equipped at position E with emergency arresting gear to provide a means of stopping military aircraft.
B — Takeoffs may be started at position A on Runway 12, and the landing portion of this runway begins at position B.
C — The takeoff and landing portion of Runway 12 begins at position B.

173. PLT077
(Refer to figure 49)
What is the difference between area A and area E on the airport depicted?

A — "A" may be used for taxi and takeoff; "E" may be used only as an overrun.
B — "A" may be used for all operations except heavy aircraft landings; "E" may be used only as an overrun.
C — "A" may be used only for taxiing; "E" may be used for all operations except landings.

174. PLT077
(Refer to figure 49)
Area C on the airport depicted is classified as a

A — stabilized area.
B — multiple heliport.
C — closed runway.

175. PLT141
(Refer to figure 50)
The arrows that appear on the end of the north/south runway indicate that the area

A — may be used only for taxiing.
B — is usable for taxiing, takeoff, and landing.
C — cannot be used for landing, but may be used for taxiing and takeoff.

176. PLT141
The numbers 9 and 27 on a runway indicate that the runway is oriented approximately

A — 009° and 027° true.
B — 090° and 270° true.
C — 090° and 270° magnetic.

177. PLT077
(Refer to figure 50)
Select the proper traffic pattern and runway for landing.

A — Left-hand traffic and Runway 18.
B — Right-hand traffic and Runway 18.
C — Left-hand traffic and Runway 22.

178. PLT077
(Refer to figure 50)
If the wind is as shown by the landing direction indicator, the pilot should land on

A — Runway 18 and expect a crosswind from the right.
B — Runway 22 directly into the wind.
C — Runway 36 and expect a crosswind from the right.

179. PLT039
(Refer to figure 51)
The segmented circle indicates that the airport traffic is

A — left-hand for Runway 18 and right-hand for Runway 36.
B — right-hand for Runway 9 and left-hand for Runway 27.
C — left-hand for Runway 36 and right-hand for Runway 18.

180. PLT039
(Refer to figure 51)
The traffic patterns indicated in the segmented circle have been arranged to avoid flights over an area to the

A — south of the airport.
B — north of the airport.
C — southeast of the airport.

181. PLT039
(Refer to figure 51)
The segmented circle indicates that a landing on Runway 26 will be with a

A — right-quartering headwind.
B — left-quartering headwind.
C — right-quartering tailwind.

182. PLT039
(Refer to figure 51)
Which runway and traffic pattern should be used as indicated by the wind cone in the segmented circle?

A — Right-hand traffic on Runway 18.
B — Left-hand traffic on Runway 36.
C — Right-hand traffic on Runway 9.

183. PLT140
Who should not participate in the Land and Hold Short Operations (LAHSO) program?

A — Recreational pilots only.
B — Military pilots.
C — Student pilots.

184. PLT140
Who has final authority to accept or decline any land and hold short (LAHSO) clearance?

A — Pilot-in-command.
B — Owner/operator.
C — Second-in-command.

185. PLT140
When should pilots decline a land and hold short (LAHSO) clearance?

A — When it will compromise safety.
B — Only when the tower operator concurs.
C — Pilots can not decline clearance.

186. PLT078
Where is the "Available Landing Distance" (ALD) data published for an airport that utilizes Land and Hold Short Operations (LAHSO) published?

A — Special Notices section of the Airport Facility Directory (A/FD).
B — 14 CFR Part 91, General Operating and Flight Rules.
C — Aeronautical Information Manual (AIM).

187. PLT140
What is the minimum visibility for a pilot to receive a land and hold short (LAHSO) clearance?

A — 3 nautical miles
B — 3 statute miles.
C — 1 statute mile.

188. PLT141
When approaching taxiway holding lines from the side with the continuous lines, the pilot

A — may continue taxiing.
B — should not cross the lines without ATC clearance.
C — should continue taxiing until all parts of the aircraft have crossed the lines.

189. PLT141
The numbers 8 and 26 on the approach ends of the runway indicate that the runway is orientated approximately

A — 008° and 026° true.
B — 080° and 260° true.
C — 080° and 260° magnetic.

190. PLT150
The recommended entry position to an airport traffic pattern is

A — 45° to the base leg just below traffic pattern altitude.
B — to enter 45° at the midpoint of the downwind leg at traffic pattern altitude.
C — to cross directly over the airport at traffic pattern altitude and join the downwind leg.

191. PLT141
What is the purpose of the runway/runway hold position sign?

A — Denotes entrance to runway from a taxiway.
B — Denotes area protected for an aircraft approaching or departing a runway.
C — Denotes intersecting runways.

192. PLT141
What does the outbound destination sign identify?

A — Identifies entrance to the runway from a taxiway.
B — Identifies direction to take-off runways.
C — Identifies runway on which an aircraft is located.

193. PLT435
If a control tower and an FSS are located on the same airport, which function is provided by the FSS during those periods when the tower is closed?

A — Automatic closing of the IFR flight plan.
B — Approach control services.
C — Airport Advisory Service.

194. PLT222
When should pilots state their position on the airport when calling the tower for takeoff?

A — When visibility is less than 1 mile.
B — When parallel runways are in use.
C — When departing from a runway intersection.

195. PLT064
(Refer to figure 21)
(Area 3) Determine the approximate latitude and longitude of Currituck County Airport.

A — 36°24'N - 76°01'W.
B — 36°48'N - 76°01'W.
C — 47°24'N - 75°58'W.

196. PLT064
(Refer to figure 22)
(Area 2) Which airport is located at approximately 47°39'30"N latitude and 100°53'00"W longitude?

A — Linrud.
B — Crooked Lake.
C — Johnson.

197. PLT064
(Refer to figure 22)
(Area 2) The CTAF/MULTICOM frequency for Garrison Airport is

A — 123.0 MHz.
B — 122.8 MHz
C — 122.9 MHz.

198. PLT064
(Refer to figure 23, 32)
(Area 2) At Coeur D'Alene, which frequency should be used as a Common Traffic Advisory Frequency (CTAF) to self-announce position and intentions?

A — 122.05 MHz.
B — 122.1/108.8 MHz.
C — 122.8 MHz.

199. PLT064
(Refer to figure 23, 32)
(Area 2) At Coeur D'Alene, which frequency should be used as a Common Traffic Advisory Frequency (CTAF) to monitor airport traffic?

A — 122.05 MHz.
B — 122.8 MHz.
C — 135.075 MHz

200. PLT064
(Refer to figure 23, 32)
(Area 2) What is the correct UNICOM frequency to be used at Coeur D'Alene to request fuel?

A — 122.1/108.8 MHz.
B — 122.8 MHz.
C — 135.075 MHz.

201. PLT064
(Refer to figure 26)
(Area 3) If Redbird Tower is not in operation, which frequency should be used as a Common Traffic Advisory Frequency (CTAF) to monitor airport traffic?

A — 120.3 MHz.
B — 122.95 MHz.
C — 126.35 MHz.

202. PLT064
(Refer to figure 27)
(Area 4) The CTAF/UNICOM frequency at Jamestown Airport is

A — 122.0 MHz.
B — 123.0 MHz.
C — 123.6 MHz.

203. PLT064
(Refer to figure 27)
(Area 6) What is the CTAF/UNICOM frequency at Barnes County Airport?

A — 122.0 MHz.
B — 122.8 MHz.
C — 123.6 MHz.

204. PLT376
(Refer to figure 27)
(Area 3) When flying over Arrowwood National Wildlife Refuge, a pilot should fly no lower than

A — 2,000 feet AGL.
B — 2,500 feet AGL.
C — 3,000 feet AGL.

205. PLT064
(Refer to figure 22)
On what frequency can a pilot receive Hazardous Inflight Weather Advisory Service (HIWAS) in the vicinity of area 1?

A — 122.0 MHz.
B — 118.0 MHz.
C — 117.1 MHz.

206. PLT064
(Refer to figure 21)
(Area 5) The CAUTION box denotes what hazard to aircraft?

A — Unmarked balloon on cable to 3,000 feet MSL.
B — Unmarked balloon on cable to 3,000 feet AGL.
C — Unmarked blimp hangers at 300 feet MSL.

207. PLT064
(Refer to figure 21)
(Area 2) The flag symbol at Lake Drummond represents a

A — compulsory reporting point for the Norfolk Class C Airspace.
B — compulsory reporting point for Hampton Roads Airport.
C — visual checkpoint used to identify position for initial callup to Norfolk Approach Control.

208. PLT064
(Refer to figure 21)
(Area 2) The elevation of the Chesapeake Regional Airport is

A — 20 feet.
B — 360 feet.
C — 36 feet.

209. PLT012
(Refer to figure 22)
The terrain elevation of the light tan area between Minot (area 1) and Audubon Lake (area 2) varies from

A — sea level to 2,000 feet MSL.
B — 2,000 feet to 2,500 feet MSL.
C — 2,000 feet to 2,700 feet MSL.

210. PLT064
(Refer to figure 22)
Which public use airports depicted are indicated as having fuel?

A — Minot Intl. (area 1) and Garrison (area 2).
B — Minot Intl. (area 1) and Mercer County Regional Airport (area 3).
C — Mercer County Regional Airport (area 3) and Garrison (area 2).

211. PLT064
(Refer to figure 24)
The flag symbols at Statesboro Bullock County Airport, Claxton-Evans County Airport, and Ridgeland Airport are

A — airports with special traffic patterns.
B — outer boundaries of Savannah Class C airspace.
C — visual checkpoints to identify position for initial callup prior to entering Savannah Class C airspace.

212. PLT064
(Refer to figure 24)
(Area 3) What is the height of the lighted obstacle approximately 6 nautical miles southwest of Savannah International?

A — 1,500 feet MSL.
B — 1,531 feet AGL.
C — 1,549 feet MSL.

213. PLT064
(Refer to figure 24)
(Area 3) The top of the group obstruction approximately 11 nautical miles from the Savannah VORTAC on the 340° radial is

A — 400 feet AGL.
B — 455 feet MSL.
C — 432 feet MSL.

214. PLT064
(Refer to figure 25)
(Area 1) What minimum altitude is necessary to vertically clear the obstacle on the northeast side of Airpark East Airport by 500 feet?

A — 1,010 feet MSL.
B — 1,273 feet MSL.
C — 1,283 feet MSL.

215. PLT064
(Refer to figure 25)
(Area 2) What minimum altitude is necessary to vertically clear the obstacle on the southeast side of Winnsboro Airport by 500 feet?

A — 823 feet MSL.
B — 1,013 feet MSL.
C — 1,403 feet MSL.

216. PLT101
(Refer to figure 26)
(Area 2) The control tower frequency for Addison Airport is

A — 122.95 MHz.
B — 126.0 MHz.
C — 133.4 MHz

217. PLT101
(Refer to figure 26)
(Area 8) What minimum altitude is required to fly over the Cedar Hill TV towers in the congested area south of NAS Dallas?

A — 2,555 feet MSL.
B — 3,349 feet MSL.
C — 3,449 feet MSL.

218. PLT064
(Refer to figure 26)
(Area 5) The navigation facility at Dallas-Ft. Worth International (DFW) is a

A — VOR.
B — VORTAC.
C — VOR/DME.

219. PLT064
Pilots flying over a national wildlife refuge are requested to fly no lower than

A — 1,000 feet AGL.
B — 2,000 feet AGL.
C — 3,000 feet AGL.

220. PLT064
Which is true concerning the blue and magenta colors used to depict airports on Sectional Aeronautical Charts?

A — Airports with control towers underlying Class A, B, and C airspace are shown in blue, Class D and E airspace are magenta.
B — Airports with control towers underlying Class C, D, and E airspace are shown in magenta
C — Airports with control towers underlying Class B, C, D, and E airspace are shown in blue.

221. PLT064
Which statement about longitude and latitude is true?

A — Lines of longitude are parallel to the Equator.
B — Lines of longitude cross the Equator at right angles.
C — The 0° line of latitude passes through Greenwich, England.

222. PLT040
(Refer to figure 27)
(Area 2.) The day VFR visibility and cloud clearance requirements to operate over the town of Cooperstown, after departing and climbing out of the Cooperstown Airport at or below 700 feet AGL are

A — 3 miles and clear of clouds.
B — 1 mile and 1,000 feet above, 500 feet below, and 2,000 feet horizontally from clouds.
C — 1 mile and clear of clouds.

223. PLT161
Unless otherwise specified, Federal Airways include that Class E airspace extending upward from

A — 700 feet above the surface up to and including 17,999 feet MSL.
B — 1,200 feet above the surface up to and including 17,999 feet MSL.
C — the surface up to and including 18,000 feet MSL.

224. PLT163
Normal VFR operations in Class D airspace with an operating control tower require the ceiling and visibility to be at least

A — 1,000 feet and 1 mile
B — 1,000 feet and 3 miles
C — 2,500 feet and 3 miles

225. PLT163
At what altitude shall the altimeter be set to 29.92, when climbing to cruising flight level?

A — 14,500 feet MSL.
B — 18,000 feet MSL.
C — 24,000 feet MSL.

226. PLT040
A blue segmented circle on a Sectional Chart depicts which class airspace?

A — Class B
B — Class C
C — Class D

227. PLT163
Airspace at an airport with a part-time control tower is classified as Class D airspace only

A — when the weather minimums are below basic VFR.
B — when the associated control tower is in operation.
C — when the associated Flight Service Station is in operation.

228. PLT434
Unless otherwise authorized, two-way radio communications with Air Traffic Control are required for landings or takeoffs.

A — at all tower controlled airports regardless of weather conditions.
B — at all tower controlled airports only when weather conditions are less than VFR.
C — at all tower controlled airports within Class D airspace only when weather conditions are less than VFR.

229. PLT434
Two-way radio communication must be established with the Air Traffic Control facility having jurisdiction over the area prior to entering which class airspace?

A — Class C
B — Class E
C — Class G

230. PLT434
What minimum radio equipment is required for operation within Class C airspace?

A — Two-way radio communications equipment and a 4096-code transponder.
B — Two-way radio communications equipment, a 4096-code transponder, and DME.
C — Two-way radio communications equipment, a 4096-code transponder, and an encoding altimeter.

231. PLT161
What minimum pilot certification is required for operation within Class B airspace?

A — Recreational Pilot Certificate.
B — Private Pilot Certificate or Student Pilot Certificate with appropriate logbook endorsements.
C — Private Pilot Certificate with an instrument rating.

232. PLT161
What minimum pilot certification is required for operation within Class B airspace?

A — Private Pilot Certificate or Student Pilot Certificate with appropriate logbook endorsements.
B — Commercial Pilot Certificate.
C — Private Pilot Certificate with an instrument rating.

233. PLT161
What minimum radio equipment is required for VFR operation within Class B airspace?

A — Two-way radio communications equipment and a 4096-code transponder.
B — Two-way radio communications equipment, a 4096-code transponder, and an encoding altimeter.
C — Two-way radio communications equipment, a 4096-code transponder, an encoding altimeter, and a VOR or TACAN receiver.

234. PLT161
An operable 4096-code transponder and Mode C encoding altimeter are required in

A — Class B airspace and within 30 miles of the Class B primary airport.
B — Class D airspace.
C — Class E airspace below 10,000 feet MSL.

235. PLT161
In which type of airspace are VFR flights prohibited?

A — Class A
B — Class B
C — Class C

236. PLT434
During operations within controlled airspace at altitudes of less than 1,200 feet AGL, the minimum horizontal distance from clouds requirement for VFR flight is

A — 1,000 feet.
B — 1,500 feet.
C — 2,000 feet.

237. PLT016
What minimum visibility and clearance from clouds are required for VFR operations in Class G airspace at 700 feet AGL or below during daylight hours?

A — 1 mile visibility and clear of clouds.
B — 1 mile visibility, 500 feet below, 1,000 feet above, and 2,000 feet horizontal clearance from clouds.
C — 3 miles visibility and clear of clouds.

238. PLT016
What minimum flight visibility is required for VFR flight operations on an airway below 10,000 feet MSL?

A — 1 mile.
B — 3 miles.
C — 4 miles.

239. PLT163
The minimum distance from clouds required for VFR operations on an airway below 10,000 feet MSL is

A — remain clear of clouds.
B — 500 feet below, 1,000 feet above, and 2,000 feet horizontally.
C — 500 feet above, 1,000 feet below, and 2,000 feet horizontally.

240. PLT163
During operations within controlled airspace at altitudes of more than 1,200 feet AGL, but less than 10,000 feet MSL, the minimum distance above clouds requirement for VFR flight is

A — 500 feet.
B — 1,000 feet.
C — 1,500 feet.

241. PLT163
VFR flight in controlled airspace above 1,200 feet AGL and below 10,000 feet MSL requires a minimum visibility and vertical cloud clearance of

A — 3 miles, and 500 feet below or 1,000 feet above the clouds in controlled airspace.
B — 5 miles, and 1,000 feet below or 1,000 feet above the clouds at all altitudes.
C — 5 miles, and 1,000 feet below or 1,000 feet above the clouds only in Class A airspace.

242. PLT163
During operations outside controlled airspace at altitudes of more than 1,200 feet AGL, but less than 10,000 feet MSL, the minimum flight visibility for VFR flight at night is

A — 1 mile.
B — 3 miles.
C — 5 miles.

243. PLT163
Outside controlled airspace, the minimum flight visibility requirement for VFR flight above 1,200 feet AGL and below 10,000 feet MSL during daylight hours is

A — 1 mile.
B — 3 miles.
C — 5 miles.

244. PLT163
During operations outside controlled airspace at altitudes of more than 1,200 feet AGL, but less than 10,000 feet MSL, the minimum distance below clouds requirement for VFR flight at night is

A — 500 feet.
B — 1,000 feet.
C — 1,500 feet.

245. PLT163
The minimum flight visibility required for VFR flights above 10,000 feet MSL and more than 1,200 feet AGL in controlled airspace is

A — 1 mile.
B — 3 miles.
C — 5 miles.

246. PLT163
For VFR flight operations above 10,000 feet MSL and more than 1,200 feet AGL, the minimum horizontal distance from clouds required is

A — 1,000 feet.
B — 2,000 feet.
C — 1 mile.

247. PLT163
During operations at altitudes of more than 1,200 feet AGL and at or above 10,000 feet MSL, the minimum distance above clouds requirement for VFR flight is

A — 500 feet.
B — 1,000 feet.
C — 1,500 feet.

248. PLT163
No person may take off or land an aircraft under basic VFR at an airport that lies within Class D airspace unless the

A — flight visibility at that airport is at least 1 mile.
B — ground visibility at that airport is at least 1 mile.
C — ground visibility at that airport is at least 3 miles.

249. PLT163
The basic VFR weather minimums for operating an aircraft within Class D airspace are

A — 500-foot ceiling and 1 mile visibility.
B — 1,000-foot ceiling and 3 miles visibility.
C — clear of clouds and 2 miles visibility.

250. PLT163
A special VFR clearance authorizes the pilot of an aircraft to operate VFR while within Class D airspace when the visibility is

A — less than 1 mile and the ceiling is less than 1,000 feet.
B — at least 1 mile and the aircraft can remain clear of clouds.
C — at least 3 miles and the aircraft can remain clear of clouds.

251. PLT163
What is the minimum weather condition required for airplanes operating under special VFR in Class D airspace?

A — 1 mile flight visibility.
B — 1 mile flight visibility and 1,000-foot ceiling.
C — 3 miles flight visibility and 1,000-foot ceiling.

252. PLT161
What are the minimum requirements for airplane operations under special VFR in Class D airspace at night?

A — The airplane must be under radar surveillance at all times while in Class D airspace.
B — The airplane must be equipped for IFR and with an altitude reporting transponder.
C — The pilot must be instrument rated, and the airplane must be IFR equipped.

253. PLT161
No person may operate an airplane within Class D airspace at night under special VFR unless the

A — flight can be conducted 500 feet below the clouds.
B — airplane is equipped for instrument flight.
C — flight visibility is at least 3 miles.

254. PLT161
An operable 4096-code transponder with an encoding altimeter is required in which airspace?

A — Class A, Class B (and within 30 miles of the Class B primary airport), and Class C.
B — Class D and Class E (below 10,000 feet MSL).
C — Class D and Class G (below 10,000 feet MSL).

255. PLT161
With certain exceptions, all aircraft within 30 miles of a Class B primary airport from the surface upward to 10,000 feet MSL must be equipped with

A — an operable VOR or TACAN receiver and an ADF receiver.
B — instruments and equipment required for IFR operations.
C — an operable transponder having either Mode S or 4096-code capability with Mode C automatic altitude reporting capability.

256. PLT040
(Refer to figure 26)
(Area 4.) The floor of Class B airspace overlying Hicks Airport (T67) north-northwest of Fort Worth Meacham Field is

A — at the surface
B — 3,200 feet MSL
C — 4,000 feet MSL

257. PLT040
(Refer to figure 26)
(Area 2.) The floor of Class B airspace at Addison Airport is

A — at the surface
B — 3,000 feet MSL
C — 3,100 feet MSL

258. PLT064
(Refer to figure 21)
(Area 4.) What hazards to aircraft may exist in restricted areas such as R-5302B?

A — Military training activities that necessitate acrobatic or abrupt flight maneuvers.
B — Unusual, often invisible, hazards such as aerial gunnery or guided missiles.
C — High volume of pilot training or an unusual type of aerial activity.

259. PLT393
(Refer to figure 27)
(Area 2) What hazards to aircraft may exist in areas such as Devils Lake East MOA?

A — Military training activities that necessitate acrobatic or abrupt flight maneuvers.
B — High volume of pilot training or an unusual type of aerial activity.
C — Unusual, often invisible, hazards to aircraft such as artillery firing, aerial gunnery, or guided missiles.

260. PLT064
(Refer to figure 22)
(Area 3) What type military flight operations should a pilot expect along IR 644?

A — VFR training flights above 1,500 feet AGL at speeds less than 250 knots.
B — IFR training flights above 1,500 feet AGL at speeds in excess of 250 knots.
C — Instrument training flights below 1,500 feet AGL at speeds in excess of 150 knots.

261. PLT163
(Refer to figure 23)
(Area 1) The visibility and cloud clearance requirements to operate VFR during daylight hours over Sandpoint Airport at 1,200 feet AGL are

A — 1 mile and 1,000 feet above, 500 feet below, and 2,000 feet horizontally from each cloud.
B — 1 mile and clear of clouds.
C — 3 miles and 1,000 feet above, 500 feet below, and 2,000 feet horizontally from each cloud.

262. PLT163
(Refer to figure 27)
(Area 2) The visibility and cloud clearance requirements to operate VFR during daylight hours over the town of Cooperstown between 1,200 feet AGL and 10,000 feet MSL are

A — 3 miles and 1,000 feet above, 500 feet below, and 2,000 feet horizontally from clouds
B — 1 mile and clear of clouds.
C — 1 mile and 1,000 feet above, 500 feet below, and 2,000 feet horizontally from clouds.

263. PLT161
(Refer to figure 27)
(Area 1) Identify the airspace over Lowe Airport.

A — Class G airspace - surface up to but not including 700 feet MSL, Class E airspace - 700 feet to 14,500 feet MSL.
B — Class G airspace - surface up to but not including 1,200 feet AGL, Class E airspace - 1,200 feet AGL up to but not including 18,000 feet MSL.
C — Class G airspace - surface up to but not including 18,000 feet MSL.

264. PLT040
(Refer to figure 27)
(Area 6) The airspace overlying and within 5 miles of Barnes County Airport is

A — Class D airspace from the surface to the floor of the overlying Class E airspace.
B — Class E airspace from the surface to 1,200 feet MSL.
C — Class G airspace from the surface to 700 feet AGL.

265. PLT101
(Refer to figure 26)
The airspace overlying Mc Kinney (TKI) is controlled from the surface to

A — 2,900 feet MSL.
B — 2,500 feet MSL.
C — 700 feet AGL.

266. PLT101
(Refer to figure 26)
(Area 4) The airspace directly overlying Fort Worth Meacham is

A — Class B airspace to 10,000 feet MSL.
B — Class C airspace to 5,000 feet MSL.
C — Class D airspace to 3,200 feet MSL.

267. PLT161
(Refer to figure 24)
(Area 3) What is the floor of the Savannah Class C airspace at the shelf area (outer circle)?

A — 1,300 feet AGL
B — 1,300 feet MSL
C — 1,700 feet MSL

268. PLT064
(Refer to figure 21)
(Area 1) What minimum radio equipment is required to land and take off at Norfolk International?

A — Mode C transponder and omnireceiver.
B — Mode C transponder and two-way radio.
C — Mode C transponder, omnireceiver, and DME.

269. PLT064
(Refer to figure 26)
At which airports is fixed-wing Special VFR not authorized?

A — Fort Worth Meacham and Fort Worth Spinks.
B — Dallas-Fort Worth International and Dallas Love Field.
C — Addison and Redbird.

270. PLT064
(Refer to figure 23)
(Area 3) The vertical limits of that portion of Class E airspace designated as a Federal Airway over Magee Airport are

A — 1,200 feet AGL to 17,999 feet MSL.
B — 7,500 feetMSL to 17,999 feet MSL.
C — 700 feet MSL to 12,500 feet MSL.

271. PLT161
The vertical limit of Class C airspace above the primary airport is normally

A — 1,200 feet AGL.
B — 3,000 feet AGL.
C — 4,000 feet AGL.

272. PLT161
The normal radius of the outer area of Class C airspace is

A — 5 nautical miles.
B — 15 nautical miles.
C — 20 nautical miles.

273. PLT161
Under what condition may an aircraft operate from a satellite airport within Class C airspace?

A — The pilot must file a flight plan prior to departure.
B — The pilot must monitor ATC until clear of the Class C airspace.
C — The pilot must contact ATC as soon as practicable after takeoff.

274. PLT064
Under what condition, if any, may pilots fly through a restricted area?

A — When flying on airways with an ATC clearance.
B — With the controlling agency's authorization.
C — Regulations do not allow this.

275. PLT064
What action should a pilot take when operating under VFR in a Military Operations Area (MOA)?

A — Obtain a clearance from the controlling agency prior to entering the MOA.
B — Operate only on the airways that transverse the MOA.
C — Exercise extreme caution when military activity is being conducted.

276. PLT444
Responsibility for collision avoidance in an alert area rests with

A — the controlling agency.
B — all pilots.
C — Air Traffic Control.

277. PLT161
The lateral dimensions of Class D airspace are based on

A — the number of airports that lie within the Class D airspace.
B — 5 statute miles from the geographical center of the primary airport.
C — the instrument procedures for which the controlled airspace is established.

278. PLT435
A non-tower satellite airport, within the same Class D airspace as that designated for the primary airport, requires radio communications be established and maintained with the

A — satellite airport's UNICOM.
B — associated Flight Service Station.
C — primary airport's control tower.

279. PLT161
Which initial action should a pilot take prior to entering Class C airspace?

A — Contact approach control on the appropriate frequency.
B — Contact the tower and request permission to enter.
C — Contact the FSS for traffic advisories.

280. PLT161
What ATC facility should the pilot contact to receive a special VFR departure clearance in Class D airspace?

A — Automated Flight Service Station.
B — Air Traffic Control Tower.
C — Air Route Traffic Control Center.

281. PLT040
Flight through a restricted area should not be accomplished unless the pilot has

A — filed an IFR flight plan.
B — received prior authorization from the controlling agency.
C — received prior permission from the commanding officer of the nearest military base.

282. PLT162
When a control tower, located on an airport within Class D airspace, ceases operation for the day, what happens to the airspace designation?

A — The airspace designation normally will not change.
B — The airspace remains Class D airspace as long as a weather observer or automated weather system is available.
C — The airspace reverts to Class E or a combination of Class E and G airspace during the hours the tower is not in operation.

283. PLT161
With certain exceptions, Class E airspace extends upward from either 700 feet or 1,200 feet AGL to, but does not include,

A — 10,000 feet MSL.
B — 14,500 feet MSL.
C — 18,000 feet MSL.

284. PLT281
Information concerning parachute jumping sites may be found in the

A — NOTAMs.
B — Airport/Facility Directory.
C — Graphic Notices and Supplemental Data.

285. PLT426
No person may use an ATC transponder unless it has been tested and inspected within at least the preceding

A — 6 calendar months.
B — 12 calendar months.
C — 24 calendar months.

286. PLT362
To use VHF/DF facilities for assistance in locating an aircraft's position, the aircraft must have a

A — VHF transmitter and receiver.
B — 4096-code transponder.
C — VOR receiver and DME.

287. PLT196
Automatic Terminal Information Service (ATIS) is the continuous broadcast of recorded information concerning

A — pilots of radar-identified aircraft whose aircraft is in dangerous proximity to terrain or to an obstruction.
B — nonessential information to reduce frequency congestion.
C — noncontrol information in selected high-activity terminal areas.

288. PLT194
An ATC radar facility issues the following advisory to a pilot flying on a heading of 090°: "TRAFFIC 3 O'CLOCK, 2 MILES, WESTBOUND..." Where should the pilot look for this traffic?

A — East.
B — South.
C — West.

289. PLT194
An ATC radar facility issues the following advisory to a pilot flying on a heading of 360°: "TRAFFIC 10 O'CLOCK, 2 MILES, SOUTHBOUND..." Where should the pilot look for this traffic?

A — Northwest.
B — Northeast.
C — Southwest.

290. PLT194
An ATC radar facility issues the following advisory to a pilot during a local flight: "TRAFFIC 2 O'CLOCK, 5 MILES, NORTHBOUND..." Where should the pilot look for this traffic?

A — Between directly ahead and 90° to the left.
B — Between directly behind and 90° to the right.
C — Between directly ahead and 90° to the right.

291. PLT194
An ATC radar facility issues the following advisory to a pilot flying north in a calm wind: "TRAFFIC 9 O'CLOCK, 2 MILES, SOUTHBOUND..." Where should the pilot look for this traffic?

A — South.
B — North.
C — West.

292. PLT172
Basic radar service in the terminal radar program is best described as

A — mandatory radar service provided by the Automated Radar Terminal System (ARTS) program.
B — safety alerts, traffic advisories, and limited vectoring to VFR aircraft.
C — wind-shear warning at participating airports.

293. PLT172
From whom should a departing VFR aircraft request radar traffic information during ground operations?

A — Clearance delivery.
B — Ground control, on initial contact.
C — Tower, just before takeoff.

294. PLT172
TRSA Service in the terminal radar program provides

A — sequencing and separation for participating VFR aircraft.
B — IFR separation (1,000 feet vertical and 3 miles lateral) between all aircraft.
C — warning to pilots when their aircraft are in unsafe proximity to terrain, obstructions, or other aircraft.

295. PLT497
When making routine transponder code changes, pilots should avoid inadvertent selection of which codes?

A — 0700, 1700, 7000.
B — 1200, 1500, 7000.
C — 7500, 7600, 7700.

296. PLT497
When operating under VFR below 18,000 feet MSL, unless otherwise authorized, what transponder code should be selected?

A — 1200.
B — 7600.
C — 7700.

297. PLT497
Unless otherwise authorized, if flying a transponder equipped aircraft, a recreational pilot should squawk which VFR code?

A — 1200.
B — 7600.
C — 7700.

298. PLT497
If Air Traffic Control advises that radar service is terminated when the pilot is departing Class C airspace, the transponder should be set to code

A — 0000.
B — 1200.
C — 4096.

299. PLT078
(Refer to figure 53)
Which type radar service is provided to VFR aircraft at Lincoln Municipal?

A — Sequencing to the primary Class C airport and standard separation.
B — Sequencing to the primary Class C airport and conflict resolution so that radar targets do not touch, or 1,000 feet vertical separation.
C — Sequencing to the primary Class C airport, traffic advisories, conflict resolution, and safety alerts.

300. PLT044
When an air traffic controller issues radar traffic information in relation to the 12-hour clock, the reference the controller uses is the aircraft's

A — true course.
B — ground track.
C — magnetic heading.

301. PLT196
Absence of the sky condition and visibility on an ATIS broadcast indicates that

A — weather conditions are at or above VFR minimums.
B — the sky condition is clear and visibility is unrestricted.
C — the ceiling is at least 5,000 feet and visibility is 5 miles or more.

302. PLT044
As Pilot in Command of an aircraft, under which situation can you deviate from an ATC clearance?

A — When operating in Class A airspace at night.
B — If an ATC clearance is not understood and in VFR conditions.
C — In response to a traffic alert and collision avoidance system resolution advisory.

303. PLT502
A steady green light signal directed from the control tower to an aircraft in flight is a signal that the pilot

A — is cleared to land.
B — should give way to other aircraft and continue circling.
C — should return for landing.

304. PLT502
Which light signal from the control tower clears a pilot to taxi?

A — Flashing green.
B — Steady green.
C — Flashing white.

305. PLT502
If the control tower uses a light signal to direct a pilot to give way to other aircraft and continue circling, the light will be

A — flashing red.
B — steady red.
C — alternating red and green.

306. PLT502
A flashing white light signal from the control tower to a taxiing aircraft is an indication to

A — taxi at a faster speed.
B — taxi only on taxiways and not cross runways.
C — return to the starting point on the airport.

307. PLT502
An alternating red and green light signal directed from the control tower to an aircraft in flight is a signal to

A — hold position.
B — exercise extreme caution.
C — not land; the airport is unsafe.

308. PLT502
While on final approach for landing, an alternating green and red light followed by a flashing red light is received from the control tower. Under these circumstances, the pilot should

A — discontinue the approach, fly the same traffic pattern and approach again, and land.
B — exercise extreme caution and abandon the approach, realizing the airport is unsafe for landing.
C — abandon the approach, circle the airport to the right, and expect a flashing white light when the airport is safe for landing.

309. PLT012
(Refer to figure 28)
An aircraft departs an airport in the eastern daylight time zone at 0945 EDT for a 2-hour flight to an airport located in the central daylight time zone. The landing should be at what coordinated universal time?

A — 1345Z.
B — 1445Z.
C — 1545Z.

310. PLT012
(Refer to figure 28)
An aircraft departs an airport in the central standard time zone at 0930 CST for a 2-hour flight to an airport located in the mountain standard time zone. The landing should be at what time?

A — 0930 MST.
B — 1030 MST.
C — 1130 MST.

311. PLT012
(Refer to figure 28)
An aircraft departs an airport in the central standard time zone at 0845 CST for a 2-hour flight to an airport located in the mountain standard time zone. The landing should be at what coordinated universal time?

A — 1345Z.
B — 1445Z.
C — 1645Z.

312. PLT012
(Refer to figure 28)
An aircraft departs an airport in the mountain standard time zone at 1615 MST for a 2-hour 15-minute flight to an airport located in the Pacific standard time zone. The estimated time of arrival at the destination airport should be

A — 1630 PST.
B — 1730 PST.
C — 1830 PST.

313. PLT012

(Refer to figure 28)
An aircraft departs an airport in the Pacific standard time zone at 1030 PST for a 4-hour flight to an airport located in the central standard time zone. The landing should be at what coordinated universal time?

A — 2030Z.
B — 2130Z.
C — 2230Z.

314. PLT012

(Refer to figure 28)
An aircraft departs an airport in the mountain standard time zone at 1515 MST for a 2-hour 30-minute flight to an airport located in the Pacific standard time zone. What is the estimated time of arrival at the destination airport?

A — 1645 PST.
B — 1745 PST.
C — 1845 PST.

315. PLT064

(Refer to figure 21)
(Area 3) What is the recommended communications procedure for a landing at Currituck County Airport?

A — Transmit intentions on 122.9 MHz when 10 miles out and give position reports in the traffic pattern.
B — Contact Elizabeth City FSS for airport advisory service.
C — Contact New Bern FSS for area traffic information.

316. PLT064

(Refer to figure 27)
(Area 2) What is the recommended communication procedure when inbound to land at Cooperstown Airport?

A — Broadcast intentions when 10 miles out on the CTAF/MULTICOM frequency, 122.9 MHz.
B — Contact UNICOM when 10 miles out on 122.8 MHz.
C — Circle the airport in a left turn prior to entering traffic.

317. PLT204

When flying HAWK N666CB, the proper phraseology for initial contact with McAlester AFSS is

A — "MC ALESTER RADIO, HAWK SIX SIX SIX CHARLIE BRAVO, RECEIVING ARDMORE VORTAC, OVER."
B — "MC ALESTER STATION, HAWK SIX SIX SIX CEE BEE, RECEIVING ARDMORE VORTAC, OVER."
C — "MC ALESTER FLIGHT SERVICE STATION, HAWK NOVEMBER SIX CHARLIE BRAVO, RECEIVING ARDMORE VORTAC, OVER."

318. PLT204

The correct method of stating 4,500 feet MSL to ATC is

A — "FOUR THOUSAND FIVE HUNDRED."
B — "FOUR POINT FIVE."
C — "FORTY-FIVE HUNDRED FEET MSL."

319. PLT204

The correct method of stating 10,500 feet MSL to ATC is

A — "TEN THOUSAND, FIVE HUNDRED FEET."
B — "TEN POINT FIVE."
C — "ONE ZERO THOUSAND, FIVE HUNDRED."

320. PLT435

Prior to entering an Airport Advisory Area, a pilot should

A — monitor ATIS for weather and traffic advisories.
B — contact approach control for vectors to the traffic pattern.
C — contact the local FSS for airport and traffic advisories.

321. PLT150

If the aircraft's radio fails, what is the recommended procedure when landing at a controlled airport?

A — Observe the traffic flow, enter the pattern, and look for a light signal from the tower.
B — Enter a crosswind leg and rock the wings.
C — Flash the landing lights and cycle the landing gear while circling the airport.

322. PLT044
After landing at a tower-controlled airport, when should the pilot contact ground control?

A — When advised by the tower to do so.
B — Prior to turning off the runway.
C — After reaching a taxiway that leads directly to the parking area.

323. PLT502
If instructed by ground control to taxi to Runway 9, the pilot may proceed

A — via taxiways and across runways to, but not onto, Runway 9.
B — to the next intersecting runway where further clearance is required.
C — via taxiways and across runways to Runway 9, where an immediate takeoff may be made.

324. PLT402
When activated, an emergency locator transmitter (ELT) transmits on

A — 118.0 and 118.8 MHz.
B — 121.5 and 243.0 MHz.
C — 123.0 and 119.0 MHz.

325. PLT402
When must the battery in an emergency locator transmitter (ELT) be replaced (or recharged if the battery is rechargeable)?

A — After one-half the battery's useful life.
B — During each annual and 100-hour inspection.
C — Every 24 calendar months.

326. PLT402
When may an emergency locator transmitter (ELT) be tested?

A — Anytime.
B — At 15 and 45 minutes past the hour.
C — During the first 5 minutes after the hour.

327. PLT402
Which procedure is recommended to ensure that the emergency locator transmitter (ELT) has not been activated?

A — Turn off the aircraft ELT after landing.
B — Ask the airport tower if they are receiving an ELT signal.
C — Monitor 121.5 before engine shutdown.

328. PLT370
An ATC clearance provides

A — priority over all other traffic.
B — adequate separation from all traffic.
C — authorization to proceed under specified traffic conditions in controlled airspace.

329. PLT078
(Refer to figure 53)
When approaching Lincoln Municipal from the west at noon for the purpose of landing, initial communications should be with

A — Lincoln Approach Control on 124.0 MHz.
B — Minneapolis Center on 128.75 MHz.
C — Lincoln Tower on 118.5 MHz.

330. PLT078
(Refer to figure 53)
What is the recommended communications procedure for landing at Lincoln Municipal during the hours when the tower is not in operation?

A — Monitor airport traffic and announce your position and intentions on 118.5 MHz.
B — Contact UNICOM on 122.95 MHz for traffic advisories.
C — Monitor ATIS for airport conditions, then announce your position on 122.95 MHz.

331. PLT435
As standard operating practice, all inbound traffic to an airport without a control tower should continuously monitor the appropriate facility from a distance of

A — 25 miles.
B — 20 miles.
C — 10 miles.

332. PLT435
(Refer to figure 23)
(Area 2) For information about the parachute jumping and glider operations at Silverwood Airport, refer to

A — notes on the border of the chart.
B — the Airport/Facility Directory.
C — the Notices to Airmen (NOTAM) publication.

333. PLT116
FAA advisory circulars (some free, others at cost) are available to all pilots and are obtained by

A — distribution from the nearest FAA district office.
B — ordering those desired from the Government Printing Office.
C — subscribing to the Federal Register.

334. PLT078
(Refer to figure 53)
Where is Loup City Municipal located with relation to the city?

A — Northeast approximately 3 miles.
B — Northwest approximately 1 mile.
C — East approximately 10 miles.

335. PLT281
The letters VHF/DF appearing in the Airport/Facility Directory for a certain airport indicate that

A — this airport is designated as an airport of entry.
B — the Flight Service Station has equipment with which to determine your direction from the station.
C — this airport has a direct-line phone to the Flight Service Station.

336. PLT078
(Refer to figure 53)
Traffic patterns in effect at Lincoln Municipal are

A — to the right on Runway 17L and Runway 35L; to the left on Runway 17R and Runway 35R.
B — to the left on Runway 17L and Runway 35L; to the right on Runway 17R and Runway 35R.
C — to the right on Runways 14 - 32.

337. PLT116
FAA advisory circulars containing subject matter specifically related to Airmen are issued under which subject number?

A — 60.
B — 70.
C — 90.

338. PLT116
FAA advisory circulars containing subject matter specifically related to Airspace are issued under which subject number?

A — 60.
B — 70.
C — 90.

339. PLT116
FAA advisory circulars containing subject matter specifically related to Air Traffic Control and General Operations are issued under which subject number?

A — 60.
B — 70.
C — 90.

340. PLT512
What causes variations in altimeter settings between weather reporting points?

A — Unequal heating of the Earth's surface.
B — Variation of terrain elevation.
C — Coriolis force.

341. PLT516
The wind at 5,000 feet AGL is southwesterly while the surface wind is southerly. This difference in direction is primarily due to

A — stronger pressure gradient at higher altitudes.
B — friction between the wind and the surface.
C — stronger Coriolis force at the surface.

342. PLT494
Convective circulation patterns associated with sea breezes are caused by

A — warm, dense air moving inland from over the water.
B — water absorbing and radiating heat faster than the land.
C — cool, dense air moving inland from over the water.

343. PLT134
How will frost on the wings of an airplane affect takeoff performance?

A — Frost will disrupt the smooth flow of air over the wing, adversely affecting its lifting capability.
B — Frost will change the camber of the wing, increasing its lifting capability.
C — Frost will cause the airplane to become airborne with a higher angle of attack, decreasing the stall speed.

344. PLT512
Every physical process of weather is accompanied by, or is the result of, a

A — movement of air.
B — pressure differential.
C — heat exchange.

345. PLT512
A temperature inversion would most likely result in which weather condition?

A — Clouds with extensive vertical development above an inversion aloft.
B — Good visibility in the lower levels of the atmosphere and poor visibility above an inversion aloft.
C — An increase in temperature as altitude is increased.

346. PLT512
The most frequent type of ground or surface-based temperature inversion is that which is produced by

A — terrestrial radiation on a clear, relatively still night.
B — warm air being lifted rapidly aloft in the vicinity of mountainous terrain.
C — the movement of colder air under warm air, or the movement of warm air over cold air.

347. PLT512
Which weather conditions should be expected beneath a low-level temperature inversion layer when the relative humidity is high?

A — Smooth air, poor visibility, fog, haze, or low clouds.
B — Light wind shear, poor visibility, haze, and light rain.
C — Turbulent air, poor visibility, fog, low stratus type clouds, and showery precipitation.

348. PLT512
What is meant by the term "dewpoint"?

A — The temperature at which condensation and evaporation are equal.
B — The temperature at which dew will always form.
C — The temperature to which air must be cooled to become saturated.

349. PLT512
The amount of water vapor which air can hold depends on the

A — dewpoint.
B — air temperature.
C — stability of the air.

350. PLT512
Clouds, fog, or dew will always form when

A — water vapor condenses.
B — water vapor is present.
C — relative humidity reaches 100 percent.

351. PLT512
What are the processes by which moisture is added to unsaturated air?

A — Evaporation and sublimation.
B — Heating and condensation.
C — Supersaturation and evaporation.

352. PLT512
Which conditions result in the formation of frost?

A — The temperature of the collecting surface is at or below freezing when small droplets of moisture fall on the surface.
B — The temperature of the collecting surface is at or below the dewpoint of the adjacent air and the dewpoint is below freezing.
C — The temperature of the surrounding air is at or below freezing when small drops of moisture fall on the collecting surface.

353. PLT512
The presence of ice pellets at the surface is evidence that there

A — are thunderstorms in the area.
B — has been cold frontal passage.
C — is a temperature inversion with freezing rain at a higher altitude.

354. PLT512
What measurement can be used to determine the stability of the atmosphere?

A — Atmospheric pressure.
B — Actual lapse rate.
C — Surface temperature.

355. PLT512
What would decrease the stability of an air mass?

A — Warming from below.
B — Cooling from below.
C — Decrease in water vapor.

356. PLT512
What is a characteristic of stable air?

A — Stratiform clouds.
B — Unlimited visibility.
C — Cumulus clouds.

357. PLT512
Moist, stable air flowing upslope can be expected to

A — produce stratus type clouds.
B — cause showers and thunderstorms.
C — develop convective turbulence.

358. PLT512
If an unstable air mass is forced upward, what type clouds can be expected?

A — Stratus clouds with little vertical development.
B — Stratus clouds with considerable associated turbulence.
C — Clouds with considerable vertical development and associated turbulence.

359. PLT512
What feature is associated with a temperature inversion?

A — A stable layer of air.
B — An unstable layer of air.
C — Chinook winds on mountain slopes.

360. PLT512
What is the approximate base of the cumulus clouds if the surface air temperature at 1,000 feet MSL is 70°F and the dewpoint is 48°F?

A — 4,000 feet MSL.
B — 5,000 feet MSL.
C — 6,000 feet MSL.

361. PLT512
At approximately what altitude above the surface would the pilot expect the base of cumuliform clouds if the surface air temperature is 82°F and the dewpoint is 38°F?

A — 9,000 feet AGL.
B — 10,000 feet AGL.
C — 11,000 feet AGL.

362. PLT512
What are characteristics of a moist, unstable air mass?

A — Cumuliform clouds and showery precipitation.
B — Poor visibility and smooth air.
C — Stratiform clouds and showery precipitation.

363. PLT512
What are characteristics of unstable air?

A — Turbulence and good surface visibility.
B — Turbulence and poor surface visibility.
C — Nimbostratus clouds and good surface visibility.

364. PLT511
A stable air mass is most likely to have which characteristic?

A — Showery precipitation.
B — Turbulent air.
C — Smooth air.

365. PLT192
The suffix "nimbus," used in naming clouds, means

A — a cloud with extensive vertical development.
B — a rain cloud.
C — a middle cloud containing ice pellets.

366. PLT192
Clouds are divided into four families according to their

A — outward shape.
B — height range.
C — composition.

367. PLT511
The boundary between two different air masses is referred to as a

A — frontolysis.
B — frontogenesis.
C — front.

368. PLT511
One of the most easily recognized discontinuities across a front is

A — a change in temperature.
B — an increase in cloud coverage.
C — an increase in relative humidity.

369. PLT511
One weather phenomenon which will always occur when flying across a front is a change in the

A — wind direction.
B — type of precipitation.
C — stability of the air mass.

370. PLT511
Steady precipitation preceding a front is an indication of

A — stratiform clouds with moderate turbulence.
B — cumuliform clouds with little or no turbulence.
C — stratiform clouds with little or no turbulence.

371. PLT226
What situation is most conducive to the formation of radiation fog?

A — Warm, moist air over low, flatland areas on clear, calm nights.
B — Moist, tropical air moving over cold, offshore water.
C — The movement of cold air over much warmer water.

372. PLT226
If the temperature/dewpoint spread is small and decreasing, and the temperature is 62°F, what type weather is most likely to develop?

A — Freezing precipitation.
B — Thunderstorms.
C — Fog or low clouds.

373. PLT226
In which situation is advection fog most likely to form?

A — A warm, moist air mass on the windward side of mountains.
B — An air mass moving inland from the coast in winter.
C — A light breeze blowing colder air out to sea.

374. PLT226
What types of fog depend upon wind in order to exist?

A — Radiation fog and ice fog.
B — Steam fog and ground fog.
C — Advection fog and upslope fog.

375. PLT226
Low-level turbulence can occur and icing can become hazardous in which type of fog?

A — Rain-induced fog.
B — Upslope fog.
C — Steam fog.

376. PLT192
An almond or lens-shaped cloud which appears stationary, but which may contain winds of 50 knots or more, is referred to as

A — an inactive frontal cloud.
B — a funnel cloud.
C — a lenticular cloud.

377. PLT192
Crests of standing mountain waves may be marked by stationary, lens-shaped clouds known as

A — mammatocumulus clouds.
B — standing lenticular clouds.
C — roll clouds.

378. PLT192
What clouds have the greatest turbulence?

A — Towering cumulus.
B — Cumulonimbus.
C — Nimbostratus.

379. PLT192
What cloud types would indicate convective turbulence?

A — Cirrus clouds.
B — Nimbostratus clouds.
C — Towering cumulus clouds.

380. PLT518
Possible mountain wave turbulence could be anticipated when winds of 40 knots or greater blow

A — across a mountain ridge, and the air is stable.
B — down a mountain valley, and the air is unstable.
C — parallel to a mountain peak, and the air is stable.

381. PLT518
Where does wind shear occur?

A — Only at higher altitudes.
B — Only at lower altitudes.
C — At all altitudes, in all directions.

382. PLT518
When may hazardous wind shear be expected?

A — When stable air crosses a mountain barrier where it tends to flow in layers forming lenticular clouds.
B — In areas of low-level temperature inversion, frontal zones, and clear air turbulence.
C — Following frontal passage when stratocumulus clouds form indicating mechanical mixing.

383. PLT518
A pilot can expect a wind-shear zone in a temperature inversion whenever the windspeed at 2,000 to 4,000 feet above the surface is at least

A — 10 knots.
B — 15 knots.
C — 25 knots.

384. PLT274
One in-flight condition necessary for structural icing to form is

A — small temperature/dewpoint spread.
B — stratiform clouds.
C — visible moisture.

385. PLT274
In which environment is aircraft structural ice most likely to have the highest accumulation rate?

A — Cumulus clouds with below freezing temperatures.
B — Freezing drizzle.
C — Freezing rain.

386. PLT274
Why is frost considered hazardous to flight?

A — Frost changes the basic aerodynamic shape of the airfoils, thereby decreasing lift.
B — Frost slows the airflow over the airfoils, thereby increasing control effectiveness.
C — Frost spoils the smooth flow of air over the wings, thereby decreasing lifting capability.

387. PLT274
How does frost affect the lifting surfaces of an airplane on takeoff?

A — Frost may prevent the airplane from becoming airborne at normal takeoff speed.
B — Frost will change the camber of the wing, increasing lift during takeoff.
C — Frost may cause the airplane to become airborne with a lower angle of attack at a lower indicated airspeed.

388. PLT192
The conditions necessary for the formation of cumulonimbus clouds are a lifting action and

A — unstable air containing an excess of condensation nuclei.
B — unstable, moist air.
C — either stable or unstable air.

389. PLT495
What feature is normally associated with the cumulus stage of a thunderstorm?

A — Roll cloud.
B — Continuous updraft.
C — Frequent lightning.

390. PLT495
Which weather phenomenon signals the beginning of the mature stage of a thunderstorm?

A — The appearance of an anvil top.
B — Precipitation beginning to fall.
C — Maximum growth rate of the clouds.

391. PLT495
What conditions are necessary for the formation of thunderstorms?

A — High humidity, lifting force, and unstable conditions.
B — High humidity, high temperature, and cumulus clouds.
C — Lifting force, moist air, and extensive cloud cover.

392. PLT495
During the life cycle of a thunderstorm, which stage is characterized predominately by downdrafts?

A — Cumulus.
B — Dissipating.
C — Mature.

393. PLT495
Thunderstorms reach their greatest intensity during the

A — mature stage.
B — downdraft stage.
C — cumulus stage.

394. PLT495
Thunderstorms which generally produce the most intense hazard to aircraft are

A — squall line thunderstorms.
B — steady-state thunderstorms.
C — warm front thunderstorms.

395. PLT495
A nonfrontal, narrow band of active thunderstorms that often develop ahead of a cold front is known as a

A — prefrontal system.
B — squall line.
C — dry line.

396. PLT495
If there is thunderstorm activity in the vicinity of an airport at which you plan to land, which hazardous atmospheric phenomenon might be expected on the landing approach?

A — Precipitation static.
B — Wind-shear turbulence.
C — Steady rain.

397. PLT501
Upon encountering severe turbulence, which flight condition should the pilot attempt to maintain?

A — Constant altitude and airspeed.
B — Constant angle of attack.
C — Level flight attitude.

398. PLT495
Which weather phenomenon is always associated with a thunderstorm?

A — Lightning.
B — Heavy rain.
C — Hail.

399. PLT509
Wingtip vortices are created only when an aircraft is

A — operating at high airspeeds.
B — heavily loaded.
C — developing lift.

400. PLT509
The greatest vortex strength occurs when the generating aircraft is

A — light, dirty, and fast.
B — heavy, dirty, and fast.
C — heavy, clean, and slow.

401. PLT509
Wingtip vortices created by large aircraft tend to

A — sink below the aircraft generating turbulence.
B — rise into the traffic pattern.
C — rise into the takeoff or landing path of a crossing runway.

402. PLT509
When taking off or landing at an airport where heavy aircraft are operating, one should be particularly alert to the hazards of wingtip vortices because this turbulence tends to

A — rise from a crossing runway into the takeoff or landing path.
B — rise into the traffic pattern area surrounding the airport.
C — sink into the flightpath of aircraft operating below the aircraft generating the turbulence.

403. PLT509
The wind condition that requires maximum caution when avoiding wake turbulence on landing is a

A — light, quartering headwind.
B — light, quartering tailwind.
C — strong headwind.

404. PLT509
When landing behind a large aircraft, the pilot should avoid wake turbulence by staying

A — above the large aircraft's final approach path and landing beyond the large aircraft's touchdown point.
B — below the large aircraft's final approach path and landing before the large aircraft's touchdown point.
C — above the large aircraft's final approach path and landing before the large aircraft's touchdown point.

405. PLT509
When departing behind a heavy aircraft, the pilot should avoid wake turbulence by maneuvering the aircraft

A — below and downwind from the heavy aircraft.
B — above and upwind from the heavy aircraft.
C — below and upwind from the heavy aircraft.

406. PLT509
When landing behind a large aircraft, which procedure should be followed for vortex avoidance?

A — Stay above its final approach flightpath all the way to touchdown.
B — Stay below and to one side of its final approach flightpath.
C — Stay well below its final approach flightpath and land at least 2,000 feet behind.

407. PLT509
How does the wake turbulence vortex circulate around each wingtip?

A — Inward, upward, and around each tip.
B — Inward, upward, and counterclockwise.
C — Outward, upward, and around each tip.

408. PLT059
(Refer to figure 12)
Which of the reporting stations have VFR weather?

A — All.
B — KINK, KBOI, and KJFK.
C — KINK, KBOI, and KLAX.

409. PLT026
For aviation purposes, ceiling is defined as the height above the Earth's surface of the

A — lowest reported obscuration and the highest layer of clouds reported as overcast.
B — lowest broken or overcast layer or vertical visibility into an obscuration.
C — lowest layer of clouds reported as scattered, broken, or thin.

410. PLT059
(Refer to figure 12)
The wind direction and velocity at KJFK is from

A — 180° true at 4 knots.
B — 180° magnetic at 4 knots.
C — 040° true at 18 knots.

411. PLT059
(Refer to figure 12)
What are the wind conditions at Wink, Texas (KINK)?

A — Calm.
B — 110° at 12 knots, peak gusts 18 knots.
C — 111° at 2 knots, peak gusts 18 knots.

412. PLT059
(Refer to figure 12)
The remarks section for KMDW has RAB35 listed. This entry means

A — blowing mist has reduced the visibility to 1-1/2 SM.
B — rain began at 1835Z.
C — the barometer has risen .35 inches Hg.

413. PLT059
(Refer to figure 12)
What are the current conditions depicted for Chicago Midway Airport (KMDW)?

A — Sky 700 feet overcast, visibility 1-1/2SM, rain.
B — Sky 7000 feet overcast, visibility 1-1/2SM, heavy rain.
C — Sky 700 feet overcast, visibility 11, occasionally 2SM, with rain.

414. PLT061
(Refer to figure 14)
The base and tops of the overcast layer reported by a pilot are

A — 1,800 feet MSL and 5,500 feet MSL.
B — 5,500 feet AGL and 7,200 feet MSL.
C — 7,200 feet MSL and 8,900 feet MSL.

415. PLT061
(Refer to figure 14)
The wind and temperature at 12,000 feet MSL as reported by a pilot are

A — 080° at 21 knots and -7°C.
B — 090° at 21 MPH and -9°F.
C — 090° at 21 knots and -9°C.

416. PLT061
(Refer to figure 14)
If the terrain elevation is 1,295 feet MSL, what is the height above ground level of the base of the ceiling?

A — 505 feet AGL.
B — 1,295 feet AGL.
C — 6,586 feet AGL.

417. PLT061
(Refer to figure 14)
The intensity of the turbulence reported at a specific altitude is

A — moderate from 5,500 feet to 7,200 feet.
B — moderate at 5,500 feet and at 7,200 feet.
C — light from 5,500 feet to 7,200 feet.

418. PLT061
(Refer to figure 14)
The intensity and type of icing reported by a pilot is

A — light to moderate rime.
B — light to moderate.
C — light to moderate clear.

419. PLT291
From which primary source should information be obtained regarding expected weather at the estimated time of arrival if your destination has no Terminal Forecast?

A — Low-Level Prognostic Chart.
B — Weather Depiction Chart.
C — Area Forecast.

420. PLT072
(Refer to figure 15)
What is the valid period for the TAF for KMEM?

A — 1200Z to 1200Z.
B — 1200Z to 1800Z.
C — 1800Z to 1800Z.

421. PLT072
(Refer to figure 15)
In the TAF for KMEM, what does "SHRA" stand for?

A — Rain showers.
B — A shift in wind direction is expected.
C — A significant change in precipitation is possible.

422. PLT072
(Refer to figure 15)
Between 1000Z and 1200Z the visibility at KMEM is forecast to be?

A — 1/2 statute mile.
B — 3 statute miles.
C — 6 statute miles.

423. PLT072
(Refer to figure 15)
What is the forecast wind for KMEM from 1600Z until the end of the forecast?

A — Variable in direction at 6 knots.
B — No significant wind.
C — Variable in direction at 4 knots.

424. PLT072
(Refer to figure 15)
In the TAF from KOKC, the "FM (FROM) Group" is forecast for the hours from 1600Z to 2200Z with the wind from

A — 180° at 10 knots, becoming 200° at 13 knots.
B — 160° at 10 knots.
C — 180° at 10 knots.

425. PLT072
(Refer to figure 15)
In the TAF from KOKC, the clear sky becomes

A — overcast at 2,000 feet during the forecast period between 2200Z and 2400Z.
B — overcast at 200 feet with a 40% probability of becoming overcast at 600 feet during the forecast period between 2200Z and 2400Z.
C — overcast at 200 feet with the probability of becoming overcast at 400 feet during the forecast period between 2200Z and 2400Z.

426. PLT072
(Refer to figure 15)
During the time period from 0600Z to 0800Z, what visibility is forecast for KOKC?

A — Greater than 6 statute miles.
B — Not forecasted.
C — Possibly 6 statute miles.

427. PLT072
(Refer to figure 15)
The only cloud type forecast in TAF reports is

A — Nimbostratus.
B — Cumulonimbus.
C — Scattered cumulus.

428. PLT291
To best determine general forecast weather conditions over several states, the pilot should refer to

A — Satellite Maps.
B — Aviation Area Forecasts.
C — Weather Depiction Charts.

429. PLT081
(Refer to figure 16)
What is the outlook for the southern half of Indiana after 0700Z?

A — VFR.
B — Scattered clouds at 3,000 feet AGL.
C — Scattered clouds at 10,000 feet.

430. PLT294
To determine the freezing level and areas of probable icing aloft, the pilot should refer to the

A — Inflight Aviation Weather Advisories.
B — Area Forecast.
C — Weather Depiction Chart.

431. PLT291
The section of the Area Forecast entitled "VFR CLDS/WX" contains a general description of

A — forecast sky cover, cloud tops, visibility, and obstructions to vision along specific routes.
B — cloudiness and weather significant to flight operations broken down by states or other geographical areas.
C — clouds and weather which cover an area greater than 3,000 square miles and is significant to VFR flight operations.

432. PLT081
(Refer to figure 16)
What sky condition and visibility are forecast for upper Michigan in the eastern portions after 2300Z?

A — Ceiling 100 feet overcast and 3 to 5 statute miles visibility.
B — Ceiling 1,000 feet overcast and 3 to 5 nautical miles visibility.
C — Ceiling 1,000 feet overcast and 3 to 5 statute miles visibility.

433. PLT081
(Refer to figure 16)
The Chicago FA forecast section is valid until the twenty-fifth at

A — 1945Z
B — 0800Z
C — 1400Z

434. PLT081
(Refer to figure 16)
What sky condition and type obstructions to vision are forecast for upper Michigan in the western portions from 0200Z until 0500Z?

A — Ceiling becoming 1,000 feet overcast with visibility 3 to 5 statute miles in mist.
B — Ceiling becoming 100 feet overcast with visibility 3 to 5 statue miles in mist.
C — Ceiling becoming 1,000 feet overcast with visibility 3 to 5 nautical miles in mist.

435. PLT067
What is indicated when a current CONVECTIVE SIGMET forecasts thunderstorms?

A — Moderate thunderstorms covering 30 percent of the area.
B — Moderate or severe turbulence.
C — Thunderstorms obscured by massive cloud layers.

436. PLT067
What information is contained in a CONVECTIVE SIGMET?

A — Tornadoes, embedded thunderstorms, and hail 3/4 inch or greater in diameter.
B — Severe icing, severe turbulence, or widespread dust storms lowering visibility to less than 3 miles.
C — Surface winds greater than 40 knots or thunderstorms equal to or greater than video integrator processor (VIP) level 4.

437. PLT067
SIGMET's are issued as a warning of weather conditions hazardous to which aircraft?

A — Small aircraft only.
B — Large aircraft only.
C — All aircraft.

438. PLT290
Which in-flight advisory would contain information on severe icing not associated with thunderstorms?

A — Convective SIGMET.
B — SIGMET.
C — AIRMET.

439. PLT290
AIRMET's are advisories of significant weather phenomena but of lower intensities than Sigmets and are intended for dissemination to

A — only IFR pilots.
B — all pilots.
C — only VFR pilots.

440. PLT076
(Refer to figure 17)
What wind is forecast for STL at 9,000 feet?

A — 230° true at 32 knots.
B — 230° magnetic at 25 knots.
C — 230° true at 25 knots

441. PLT076
What values are used for Winds Aloft Forecasts?

A — Magnetic direction and knots.
B — Magnetic direction and miles per hour.
C — True direction and knots.

442. PLT076
When the term "light and variable" is used in reference to a Winds Aloft Forecast, the coded group and windspeed is

A — 0000 and less than 7 knots.
B — 9900 and less than 5 knots.
C — 9999 and less than 10 knots.

443. PLT075
(Refer to figure 18)
What is the status of the front that extends from Nebraska through the upper peninsula of Michigan?

A — Cold.
B — Warm
C — Stationary

444. PLT075
(Refer to figure 18)
The IFR weather in northern Texas is due to

A — low ceilings.
B — dust devils.
C — intermittent rain.

445. PLT075
(Refer to figure 18)
Of what value is the Weather Depiction Chart to the pilot?

A — For determining general weather conditions on which to base flight planning.
B — For a forecast of cloud coverage, visibilities, and frontal activity.
C — For determining frontal trends and air mass characteristics.

446. PLT075
(Refer to figure 18)
The marginal weather in central Kentucky is due to low

A — visibility.
B — ceiling and visibility.
C — ceiling.

447. PLT075
(Refer to figure 18)
What weather phenomenon is causing IFR conditions in central Oklahoma?

A — Low visibility only.
B — Heavy rain Showers.
C — Low Ceilings and visibility.

448. PLT075
(Refer to figure 18)
According to the Weather Depiction Chart, the weather for a flight from southern Michigan to north Indiana is ceilings

A — 1,000 to 3,000 feet and/or visibility 3 to 5 miles.
B — less than 1,000 feet and/or visibility less than 3 miles.
C — greater than 3, 000 feet and visibility greater than 5 miles.

449. PLT037
Radar weather reports are of special interest to pilots because they indicate

A — location of precipitation along with type, intensity, and cell movement of precipitation.
B — location of precipitation along with type, intensity, and trend.
C — large areas of low ceilings and fog.

450. PLT353
What information is provided by the Radar Summary Chart that is not shown on other weather charts?

A — Lines and cells of hazardous thunderstorms.
B — Ceilings and precipitation between reporting stations.
C — Types of clouds between reporting stations.

451. PLT063
(Refer to figure 19)
(Area B) What is the top for precipitation of the radar return?

A — 24,000 feet AGL.
B — 2,400 feet MSL.
C — 24,000 feet MSL.

452. PLT063
(Refer to figure 19)
(Area D) What is the direction and speed of movement of the cell?

A — North at 17 knots.
B — South at 17 knots.
C — North at 17 MPH.

453. PLT063
(Refer to figure 19)
(Area E) The top of the precipitation of the cell is

A — 16,000 feet MSL.
B — 25,000 feet MSL.
C — 16,000 feet AGL.

454. PLT063
What does the heavy dashed line that forms a large rectangular box on a radar summary chart refer to?

A — Severe weather watch area.
B — Areas of hail 1/4 inch in diameter.
C — Areas of heavy rain.

455. PLT068
(Refer to figure 20)
How are Significant Weather Prognostic Charts best used by a pilot?

A — For overall planning at all altitudes.
B — For determining areas to avoid (freezing levels and turbulence).
C — For analyzing current frontal activity and cloud coverage.

456. PLT068
(Refer to figure 20)
Interpret the weather symbol depicted in Utah on the 12-hour Significant Weather Prognostic Chart.

A — Moderate turbulence, surface to 18,000 feet.
B — Base of clear air turbulence, 18,000 feet.
C — Thunderstorm tops at 18,000 feet.

457. PLT068
(Refer to figure 20)
What weather is forecast for the Florida area just ahead of the stationary front during the first 12 hours?

A — Ceiling 1,000 to 3,000 feet and/or visibility 3 to 5 miles with intermittent precipitation.
B — Ceiling 1,000 to 3,000 feet and/or visibility 3 to 5 miles with continuous precipitation.
C — Ceiling less than 1,000 feet and/or visibility less than 3 miles with continuous precipitation.

458. PLT068
(Refer to figure 20)
The enclosed shaded area associated with the low pressure system over northern Utah is forecast to have

A — continuous snow.
B — intermittent snow.
C — continuous snow showers.

459. PLT068
(Refer to figure 20)
At what altitude is the freezing level over the middle of Florida on the 12-hour Significant Weather Prognostic Chart?

A — 4,000 feet.
B — 12,000 feet.
C — 8,000 feet.

460. PLT513
Individual forecasts for specific routes of flight can be obtained from which weather source?

A — Transcribed Weather Broadcasts (TWEBs).
B — Terminal Forecasts.
C — Area Forecasts.

461. PLT513
Transcribed Weather Broadcasts (TWEBs) may be monitored by tuning the appropriate radio receiver to certain

A — airport advisory frequencies.
B — VOR and NDB frequencies.
C — ATIS frequencies.

462. PLT513
When telephoning a weather briefing facility for preflight weather information, pilots should state

A — the aircraft identification or the pilot's name.
B — true airspeed.
C — fuel on board.

463. PLT514
To get a complete weather briefing for the planned flight, the pilot should request

A — a general briefing.
B — an abbreviated briefing.
C — a standard briefing.

464. PLT514
Which type weather briefing should a pilot request, when departing within the hour, if no preliminary weather information has been received?

A — Outlook briefing.
B — Abbreviated briefing.
C — Standard briefing.

465. PLT514
Which type of weather briefing should a pilot request to supplement mass disseminated data?

A — An outlook briefing.
B — A supplemental briefing.
C — An abbreviated briefing.

466. PLT514
To update a previous weather briefing, a pilot should request

A — an abbreviated briefing.
B — a standard briefing.
C — an outlook briefing.

467. PLT514
A weather briefing that is provided when the information requested is 6 or more hours in advance of the proposed departure time is

A — an outlook briefing.
B — a forecast briefing.
C — a prognostic briefing.

468. PLT514
When requesting weather information for the following morning, a pilot should request

A — an outlook briefing.
B — a standard briefing.
C — an abbreviated briefing.

469. PLT513
To obtain a continuous transcribed weather briefing, including winds aloft and route forecasts for a cross-country flight, a pilot should monitor a

A — VHF radio receiver tuned to an Automatic Terminal Information Service (ATIS) frequency.
B — Transcribed Weather Broadcast (TWEB) on an NDB or a VOR facility.
C — regularly scheduled weather broadcast on a VOR frequency.

470. PLT513
What should pilots state initially when telephoning a weather briefing facility for preflight weather information?

A — Tell the number of occupants on board.
B — State their total flight time.
C — Identify themselves as pilots.

471. PLT513
When telephoning a weather briefing facility for preflight weather information, pilots should state

A — the full name and address of the formation commander.
B — that they possess a current pilot certificate.
C — whether they intend to fly VFR only.

472. PLT515
How should contact be established with an En Route Flight Advisory Service (EFAS) station, and what service would be expected?

A — Call EFAS on 122.2 for routine weather, current reports on hazardous weather, and altimeter settings.
B — Call flight assistance on 122.5 for advisory service pertaining to severe weather.
C — Call Flight Watch on 122.0 for information regarding actual weather and thunderstorm activity along proposed route.

473. PLT515
What service should a pilot normally expect from an En Route Flight Advisory Service (EFAS) station?

A — Actual weather information and thunderstorm activity along the route.
B — Preferential routing and radar vectoring to circumnavigate severe weather.
C — Severe weather information, changes to flight plans, and receipt of routine position reports.

474. PLT515
Below FL180, en route weather advisories should be obtained from an FSS on

A — 122.0 MHz.
B — 122.1 MHz.
C — 123.6 MHz.

475. PLT506
Which would provide the greatest gain in altitude in the shortest distance during climb after takeoff?

A — V_Y
B — V_A
C — V_X

476. PLT506
After takeoff, which airspeed would the pilot use to gain the most altitude in a given period of time?

A — V_Y
B — V_X
C — V_A

477. PLT127
What effect does high density altitude, as compared to low density altitude, have on propeller efficiency and why?

A — Efficiency is increased due to less friction on the propeller blades.
B — Efficiency is reduced because the propeller exerts less force at high density altitudes than at low density altitudes.
C — Efficiency is reduced due to the increased force of the propeller in the thinner air.

478. PLT134
Which combination of atmospheric conditions will reduce aircraft takeoff and climb performance?

A — Low temperature, low relative humidity, and low density altitude.
B — High temperature, low relative humidity, and low density altitude.
C — High temperature, high relative humidity, and high density altitude.

479. PLT127
What effect does high density altitude have on aircraft performance?

A — It increases engine performance.
B — It reduces climb performance.
C — It increases takeoff performance.

480. PLT127
What effect, if any, does high humidity have on aircraft performance?

A — It increases performance.
B — It decreases performance.
C — It has no effect on performance.

481. PLT012
(Refer to figure 36)
Approximately what true airspeed should a pilot expect with 65 percent maximum continuous power at 9,500 feet with a temperature of 36°F below standard?

A — 178 MPH.
B — 181 MPH.
C — 183 MPH.

482. PLT012
(Refer to figure 36)
What is the expected fuel consumption for a 1,000-nautical mile flight under the following conditions?

Pressure altitude...8,000 ft
Temperature...22°C
Manifold pressure...20.8 inches Hg.
Wind...Calm.

A — 60.2 gallons.
B — 70.1 gallons.
C — 73.2 gallons.

483. PLT012
(Refer to figure 36)
What fuel flow should a pilot expect at 11,000 feet on a standard day with 65 percent maximum continuous power?

A — 10.6 gallons per hour.
B — 11.2 gallons per hour.
C — 11.8 gallons per hour.

484. PLT012
(Refer to figure 36)
Determine the approximate manifold pressure setting with 2,450 RPM to achieve 65 percent maximum continuous power at 6,500 feet with a temperature of 36°F higher than standard.

A — 19.8 inches Hg.
B — 20.8 inches Hg.
C — 21.0 inches Hg.

485. PLT013
(Refer to figure 37)
What is the headwind component for a landing on Runway 18 if the tower reports the wind as 220° at 30 knots?

A — 19 knots.
B — 23 knots.
C — 26 knots.

486. PLT013
(Refer to figure 37)
Determine the maximum wind velocity for a 45° crosswind if the maximum crosswind component for the airplane is 25 knots.

A — 25 knots.
B — 29 knots.
C — 35 knots.

487. PLT013
(Refer to figure 37)
What is the maximum wind velocity for a 30° crosswind if the maximum crosswind component for the airplane is 12 knots?

A — 16 knots.
B — 20 knots.
C — 24 knots.

488. PLT013
(Refer to figure 37)
With a reported wind of north at 20 knots, which runway (6, 29, or 32) is acceptable for use for an airplane with a 13-knot maximum crosswind component?

A — Runway 6.
B — Runway 29.
C — Runway 32.

489. PLT013
(Refer to figure 37)
With a reported wind of south at 20 knots, which runway (10, 14, or 24) is appropriate for an airplane with a 13-knot maximum crosswind component?

A — Runway 10.
B — Runway 14.
C — Runway 24.

490. PLT013
(Refer to figure 37)
What is the crosswind component for a landing on Runway 18 if the tower reports the wind as 220° at 30 knots?

A — 19 knots.
B — 23 knots.
C — 30 knots.

491. PLT008
(Refer to figure 38)
Determine the approximate total distance required to land over a 50-foot obstacle.

OAT...90°F
Pressure altitude...4,000 ft
Weight...2,800 lb
Headwind component...10 kts

A — 1,525 feet.
B — 1,950 feet.
C — 1,775 feet.

492. PLT008
(Refer to figure 39)
Determine the approximate landing ground roll distance.

Pressure altitude...Sea level
Headwind...4 kts
Temperature...Std

A — 356 feet.
B — 401 feet.
C — 490 feet.

493. PLT008
(Refer to figure 39)
Determine the total distance required to land over a 50-foot obstacle.

Pressure altitude...7,500 ft
Headwind...8 kts
Temperature...32°F
Runway...Hard surface

A — 1,004 feet.
B — 1,205 feet.
C — 1,506 feet.

494. PLT008
(Refer to figure 39)
Determine the total distance required to land over a 50-foot obstacle.

Pressure altitude...5,000 ft
Headwind...8 kts
Temperature...41°F
Runway...Hard surface

A — 837 feet.
B — 956 feet.
C — 1,076 feet.

495. PLT008
(Refer to figure 39)
Determine the approximate landing ground roll distance.

Pressure altitude...5,000 ft
Headwind...Calm
Temperature...101°F

A — 495 feet.
B — 545 feet.
C — 445 feet.

496. PLT008
(Refer to figure 39)
Determine the total distance required to land over a 50-foot obstacle.

Pressure altitude...3,750 ft
Headwind...12 kts
Temperature...Std

A — 794 feet.
B — 836 feet.
C — 816 feet.

497. PLT008
(Refer to figure 39)
Determine the approximate landing ground roll distance.

Pressure altitude...1,250 ft
Headwind...8 kts
Temperature...Std

A — 275 feet.
B — 366 feet.
C — 470 feet.

498. PLT208
If an emergency situation requires a downwind landing, pilots should expect a faster

A — airspeed at touchdown, a longer ground roll, and better control throughout the landing roll.
B — groundspeed at touchdown, a longer ground roll, and the likelihood of overshooting the desired touchdown point.
C — groundspeed at touchdown, a shorter ground roll, and the likelihood of undershooting the desired touchdown point.

499. PLT011
(Refer to figure 41)
Determine the total distance required for takeoff to clear a 50-foot obstacle.

OAT...Std
Pressure altitude...4,000 ft
Takeoff weight...2,800 lb
Headwind component...Calm

A — 1,500 feet.
B — 1,750 feet.
C — 2,000 feet.

500. PLT011
(Refer to figure 41)
Determine the total distance required for takeoff to clear a 50-foot obstacle.

OAT...Std
Pressure altitude...Sea level
Takeoff weight...2,700 lb
Headwind component...Calm

A — 1,000 feet.
B — 1,400 feet.
C — 1,700 feet.

501. PLT011
(Refer to figure 41)
Determine the approximate ground roll distance required for takeoff.

OAT...100°F
Pressure altitude...2,000 ft
Takeoff weight...2,750 lb
Headwind component...Calm

A — 1,150 feet.
B — 1,300 feet.
C — 1,800 feet.

502. PLT011
(Refer to figure 41)
Determine the approximate ground roll distance required for takeoff.

OAT...90°F
Pressure altitude...2,000 ft
Takeoff weight...2,500 lb
Headwind component...20 kts

A — 650 feet.
B — 800 feet.
C — 1,000 feet.

503. PLT208

If an emergency situation requires a downwind landing, pilots should expect a faster

A — airspeed at touchdown, a longer ground roll, and better control throughout the landing roll.
B — groundspeed at touchdown, a longer ground roll, and the likelihood of overshooting the desired touchdown point.
C — groundspeed at touchdown, a shorter ground roll, and the likelihood of undershooting the desired touchdown point.

504. PLT328

Which items are included in the empty weight of an aircraft?

A — Unusable fuel and undrainable oil
B — Only the airframe, powerplant, and optional equipment.
C — Full fuel tanks and engine oil to capacity.

505. PLT328

An aircraft is loaded 110 pounds over maximum certificated gross weight. If fuel (gasoline) is drained to bring the aircraft weight within limits, how much fuel should be drained?

A — 15.7 gallons.
B — 16.2 gallons.
C — 18.4 gallons.

506. PLT328

GIVEN:

	WEIGHT (LB)	ARM (IN)	MOMENT (LB-IN)
Empty weight	1,495.0	101.4	151,593.0
Pilot and Pass	380.0	64.0	-----
Fuel (30 gal usable no reserve)	-----	96.0	-----

The CG is located how far aft of datum?

A — CG 92.44.
B — CG 94.01.
C — CG 119.8.

507. PLT328

(Refer to figure 33, 34)
What is the maximum amount of baggage that can be carried when the airplane is loaded as follows?

Front seat occupants...387 lb
Rear seat occupants...293 lb
Fuel...35 gal

A — 45 pounds.
B — 63 pounds.
C — 220 pounds.

508. PLT328
(Refer to figure 33, 34)
Determine if the airplane weight and balance is within limits.

Front seat occupants...415 lb
Rear seat occupants...110 lb
Fuel, main tanks...44 gal
Fuel, aux. tanks...19 gal
Baggage...32 lb.

A — 19 pounds overweight, CG within limits.
B — 19 pounds overweight, CG out of limits forward.
C — Weight within limits, CG out of limits.

509. PLT328
(Refer to figure 35)
What is the maximum amount of baggage that may be loaded aboard the airplane for the CG to remain within the moment envelope?

	WEIGHT (LB)	MOM/1000
Empty weight	1,350	51.5
Pilot and Front passenger	250	-----
Rear passengers	400	-----
Baggage	-----	-----
Fuel, 30 gal	-----	-----
Oil, 8 qt	-----	-0.2

A — 105 pounds.
B — 110 pounds.
C — 120 pounds.

510. PLT328
(Refer to figure 35)
Calculate the moment of the airplane and determine which category is applicable.

	WEIGHT (LB)	MOM/1000
Empty weight	1,350	51.5
Pilot and Front passenger	310	-----
Rear passengers	96	-----
Fuel, 38 gal	-----	-----
Oil, 8 qt	-----	-0.2

A — 79.2, utility category.
B — 80.8, utility category.
C — 81.2, normal category.

511. PLT328

(Refer to figure 35)

What is the maximum amount of fuel that may be aboard the airplane on takeoff if loaded as follows?

	WEIGHT (LB)	MOM/1000
Empty weight	1,350	51.5
Pilot and Front passenger	340	-----
Rear passengers	310	-----
Baggage	45	-----
Oil, 8 qt	-----	-----

A — 24 gallons.
B — 32 gallons.
C — 40 gallons.

512. PLT328

(Refer to figure 35)

Determine the moment with the following data:

	WEIGHT (LB)	MOM/1000
Empty weight	1,350	51.5
Pilot and Front passenger	340	-----
Fuel (std. tanks)	Capacity	-----
Oil, 8 qt	-----	-----

A — 69.9 pound-inches.
B — 74.9 pound-inches.
C — 77.6 pound-inches.

513. PLT328
(Refer to figure 35)
Determine the aircraft loaded moment and the aircraft category.

	WEIGHT (LB)	MOM/1000
Empty weight	1,350	51.5
Pilot and Front passenger	380	-----
Fuel, 48 gal	288	-----
Oil, 8 qt	-----	-----

A — 78.2, normal category.
B — 79.2, normal category.
C — 80.4, utility category.

514. PLT328
(Refer to figure 33, 34)
Upon landing, the front passenger (180 pounds) departs the airplane. A rear passenger (204 pounds) moves to the front passenger position. What effect does this have on the CG if the airplane weighed 2,690 pounds and the MOM/100 was 2,260 just prior to the passenger transfer?

A — The CG moves forward approximately 3 inches.
B — The weight changes, but the CG is not affected.
C — The CG moves forward approximately 0.1 inch.

515. PLT328
(Refer to figure 33, 34)
Which action can adjust the airplane's weight to maximum gross weight and the CG within limits for takeoff?

Front seat occupants...425 lb
Rear seat occupants...300 lb
Fuel, main tanks...44 gal

A — Drain 12 gallons of fuel.
B — Drain 9 gallons of fuel.
C — Transfer 12 gallons of fuel from the main tanks to the auxiliary tanks.

516. PLT328
(Refer to figure 33, 34)
What effect does a 35-gallon fuel burn (main tanks) have on the weight and balance if the airplane weighed 2,890 pounds and the MOM/100 was 2,452 at takeoff?

A — Weight is reduced by 210 pounds and the CG is aft of limits.
B — Weight is reduced by 210 pounds and the CG is unaffected.
C — Weight is reduced to 2,680 pounds and the CG moves forward.

517. PLT328
(Refer to figure 33, 34)
With the airplane loaded as follows, what action can be taken to balance the airplane?

Front seat occupants..411 lb
Rear seat occupants...100 lb
Main wing tanks...44 gal

A — Fill the auxiliary wing tanks.
B — Add a 100-pound weight to the baggage compartment.
C — Transfer 10 gallons of fuel from the main tanks to the auxiliary tanks.

518. PLT328
(Refer to figure 62)
If 50 pounds of weight is located at point X and 100 pounds at point Z, how much weight must be located at point Y to balance the plank?

A — 30 pounds.
B — 50 pounds.
C — 300 pounds.

519. PLT328
(Refer to figure 61)
How should the 500-pound weight be shifted to balance the plank on the fulcrum?

A — 1 inch to the left.
B — 1 inch to the right.
C — 4.5 inches to the right.

520. PLT005
(Refer to figure 8)
What is the effect of a temperature increase from 25 to 50°F on the density altitude if the pressure altitude remains at 5,000 feet?

A — 1,200-foot increase.
B — 1,400-foot increase.
C — 1,650-foot increase.

521. PLT005
(Refer to figure 8)
Determine the pressure altitude with an indicated altitude of 1,380 feet MSL with an altimeter setting of 28.22 at standard temperature.

A — 3,010 feet MSL.
B — 2,991 feet MSL.
C — 2,913 feet MSL.

522. PLT005
(Refer to figure 8)
Determine the density altitude for these conditions:

Altimeter setting...29.25
Runway temperature...+81°F
Airport elevation...5,250 ft MSL

A — 4,600 feet MSL.
B — 5,877 feet MSL.
C — 8,500 feet MSL.

523. PLT019
(Refer to figure 8)
Determine the pressure altitude at an airport that is 3,563 feet MSL with an altimeter setting of 29.96.

A — 3,527 feet MSL.
B — 3,556 feet MSL.
C — 3,639 feet MSL.

524. PLT005
(Refer to figure 8)
What is the effect of a temperature increase from 30 to 50°F on the density altitude if the pressure altitude remains at 3,000 feet MSL?

A — 900-foot increase.
B — 1,100-foot decrease.
C — 1,300-foot increase.

525. PLT005
(Refer to figure 8)
Determine the pressure altitude at an airport that is 1,386 feet MSL with an altimeter setting of 29.97.

A — 1,341 feet MSL.
B — 1,451 feet MSL.
C — 1,562 feet MSL.

526. PLT005
(Refer to figure 8)
What is the effect of a temperature decrease and a pressure altitude increase on the density altitude from 90°F and 1,250 feet pressure altitude to 55°F and 1,750 feet pressure altitude?

A — 1,700-foot increase.
B — 1,300-foot decrease.
C — 1,700-foot decrease.

527. PLT012
(Refer to figure 21)
En route to First Flight Airport (area 5), your flight passes over Hampton Roads Airport (area 2) at 1456 and then over Chesapeake Municipal at 1501. At what time should your flight arrive at First Flight?

A — 1516.
B — 1521.
C — 1526.

528. PLT012
(Refer to figure 22)
What is the estimated time en route from Mercer County Regional Airport (area 3) to Minot International (area 1)? The wind is from 330° at 25 knots and the true airspeed is 100 knots. Add 3-1/2 minutes for departure and climb-out.

A — 44 minutes.
B — 48 minutes.
C — 52 minutes.

529. PLT012
(Refer to figure 23)
What is the estimated time en route from Sandpoint Airport (area 1) to St. Maries Airport (area 4)? The wind is from 215° at 25 knots and the true airspeed is 125 knots.

A — 38 minutes.
B — 34 minutes.
C — 30 minutes.

530. PLT012
(Refer to figure 23)
Determine the estimated time en route for a flight from Priest River Airport (area 1) to Shoshone County Airport (area 3). The wind is from 030 at 12 knots and the true airspeed is 95 knots. Add 2 minutes for climb-out.

A — 27 minutes.
B — 29 minutes.
C — 31 minutes.

531. PLT012
(Refer to figure 23)
What is the estimated time en route for a flight from St. Maries Airport (area 4) to Priest River Airport (area 1)? The wind is from 300° at 14 knots and the true airspeed is 90 knots. Add 3 minutes for climb-out.

A — 38 minutes.
B — 43 minutes.
C — 48 minutes.

532. PLT012
(Refer to figure 24)
What is the estimated time en route for a flight from Allendale County Airport (area 1) to Claxton-Evans County Airport (area 2)? The wind is from 100° at 18 knots and the true airspeed is 115 knots. Add 2 minutes for climb-out.

A — 33 minutes.
B — 27 minutes.
C — 30 minutes.

533. PLT012
(Refer to figure 24)
What is the estimated time en route for a flight from Claxton-Evans County Airport (area 2) to Hampton Varnville Airport (area 1)? The wind is from 290° at 18 knots and the true airspeed is 85 knots. Add 2 minutes for climb-out.

A — 35 minutes.
B — 39 minutes.
C — 44 minutes.

534. PLT012

(Refer to figure 24)
While en route on Victor 185, a flight crosses the 248° radial of Allendale VOR at 0953 and then crosses the 216° radial of Allendale VOR at 1000. What is the estimated time of arrival at Savannah VORTAC?

A — 1023.
B — 1036.
C — 1028.

535. PLT012

(Refer to figure 26)
What is the estimated time en route for a flight from Denton Muni (area 1) to Addison (area 2)? The wind is from 200° at 20 knots, the true airspeed is 110 knots, and the magnetic variation is 7° east.

A — 13 minutes.
B — 16 minutes.
C — 19 minutes.

536. PLT012

(Refer to figure 26)
Estimate the time en route from Addison (area 2) to Redbird (area 3). The wind is from 300° at 15 knots, the true airspeed is 120 knots, and the magnetic variation is 7° east.

A — 8 minutes.
B — 11 minutes.
C — 14 minutes.

537. PLT012

If a true heading of 135° results in a ground track of 130° and a true airspeed of 135 knots results in a groundspeed of 140 knots, the wind would be from

A — 019° and 12 knots.
B — 200° and 13 knots.
C — 246° and 13 knots.

538. PLT012

(Refer to figure 63)
In flying the rectangular course, when would the aircraft be turned less than 90°?

A — Corners 1 and 4.
B — Corners 1 and 2.
C — Corners 2 and 4.

539. PLT219

(Refer to figure 67)
While practicing S-turns, a consistently smaller half-circle is made on one side of the road than on the other, and this turn is not completed before crossing the road or reference line. This would most likely occur in turn

A — 1-2-3 because the bank is decreased too rapidly during the latter part of the turn.
B — 4-5-6 because the bank is increased too rapidly during the early part of the turn.
C — 4-5-6 because the bank is increased too slowly during the latter part of the turn.

540. PLT012

How far will an aircraft travel in 2-1/2 minutes with a groundspeed of 98 knots?

A — 2.45 NM.
B — 3.35 NM.
C — 4.08 NM.

541. PLT012

On a cross-country flight, point A is crossed at 1500 hours and the plan is to reach point B at 1530 hours. Use the following information to determine the indicated airspeed required to reach point B on schedule.

Distance between A and B: 70 NM
Forecast wind: 310° at 15 kts
Pressure altitude: 8,000 ft
Ambient temperature: -10°C
True course: 270°

The required indicated airspeed would be approximately

A — 126 knots.
B — 137 knots.
C — 152 knots.

542. PLT467
Which cruising altitude is appropriate for a VFR flight on a magnetic course of 135°?

A — Even thousands.
B — Even thousands plus 500 feet.
C — Odd thousands plus 500 feet.

543. PLT467
Which VFR cruising altitude is acceptable for a flight on a Victor Airway with a magnetic course of 175°? The terrain is less than 1,000 feet.

A — 4,500 feet.
B — 5,000 feet.
C — 5,500 feet.

544. PLT467
Which VFR cruising altitude is appropriate when flying above 3,000 feet AGL on a magnetic course of 185°?

A — 4,000 feet.
B — 4,500 feet.
C — 5,000 feet.

545. PLT467
Each person operating an aircraft at a VFR cruising altitude shall maintain an odd-thousand plus 500-foot altitude while on a

A — magnetic heading of 0° through 179°.
B — magnetic course of 0° through 179°.
C — true course of 0° through 179°.

546. PLT012
(Refer to figure 21)
Determine the magnetic course from First Flight Airport (area 5) to Hampton Roads Airport (area 2).

A — 141°.
B — 321°.
C — 331°.

547. PLT012
(Refer to figure 22)
Determine the magnetic heading for a flight from Mercer County Regional Airport (area 3) to Minot International (area 1). The wind is from 330° at 25 knots, the true airspeed is 100 knots, and the magnetic variation is 10° east.

A — 002°.
B — 012°.
C — 352°.

548. PLT012
(Refer to figure 23)
Determine the magnetic heading for a flight from Sandpoint Airport (area 1) to St. Maries Airport (area 4). The wind is from 215° at 25 knots, and the true airspeed is 125 knots.

A — 169°.
B — 349°.
C — 187°.

549. PLT012
(Refer to figure 23)
What is the magnetic heading for a flight from Priest River Airport (area 1) to Shoshone County Airport (area 3)? The wind is from 030° at 12 knots and the true airspeed is 95 knots.

A — 143°.
B — 118°.
C — 136°.

550. PLT012
(Refer to figure 23)
Determine the magnetic heading for a flight from St. Maries Airport (area 4) to Priest River Airport (area 1). The wind is from 340° at 10 knots and the true airspeed is 90 knots.

A — 345°.
B — 320°.
C — 327°.

551. PLT012

(Refer to figure 24)
Determine the magnetic heading for a flight from Allendale County Airport (area 1) to Claxton-Evans County Airport (area 2). The wind is from 090° at 16 knots and the true airspeed is 90 knots.

A — 208°.
B — 230°.
C — 212°.

552. PLT012

(Refer to figure 24 59)
Determine the compass heading for a flight from Claxton-Evans County Airport (area 2) to Hampton Varnville Airport (area 1). The wind is from 280° at 08 knots, and the true airspeed is 85 knots.

A — 033°.
B — 042°.
C — 038°.

553. PLT012

(Refer to figure 25)
Determine the magnetic course from Airpark East Airport (area 1) to Winnsboro Airport (area 2). Magnetic variation is 6°30'E.

A — 075°.
B — 082°.
C — 091°.

554. PLT012

(Refer to figure 26)
Determine the magnetic heading for a flight from Fort Worth Meacham (area 4) to Denton Muni (area 1). The wind is from 330° at 25 knots, the true airspeed is 110 knots, and the magnetic variation is 7° east.

A — 003°.
B — 017°.
C — 023°.

555. PLT012

(Refer to figure 27)
Determine the magnetic course from Breckheimer (Pvt) Airport (area 1) to Jamestown Airport (area 4).

A — 180°.
B — 188°.
C — 360°.

556. PLT455

(Refer to figure 52)
If more than one cruising altitude is intended, which should be entered in block 7 of the flight plan?

A — Initial cruising altitude.
B — Highest cruising altitude.
C — Lowest cruising altitude.

557. PLT455

(Refer to figure 52)
What information should be entered in block 9 for a VFR day flight?

A — The name of the airport of first intended landing.
B — The name of destination airport if no stopover for more than 1 hour is anticipated.
C — The name of the airport where the aircraft is based.

558. PLT455

(Refer to figure 52)
What information should be entered in block 12 for a VFR day flight?

A — The estimated time en route plus 30 minutes.
B — The estimated time en route plus 45 minutes.
C — The amount of usable fuel on board expressed in time.

559. PLT455

How should a VFR flight plan be closed at the completion of the flight at a controlled airport?

A — The tower will automatically close the flight plan when the aircraft turns off the runway.
B — The pilot must close the flight plan with the nearest FSS or other FAA facility upon landing.
C — The tower will relay the instructions to the nearest FSS when the aircraft contacts the tower for landing.

560. PLT014
(Refer to figure 21)
What is your approximate position on low altitude airway Victor 1, southwest of Norfolk (area 1), if the VOR receiver indicates you are on the 340° radial of Elizabeth City VOR (area 3)?

A — 15 nautical miles from Norfolk VORTAC.
B — 18 nautical miles from Norfolk VORTAC.
C — 23 nautical miles from Norfolk VORTAC.

561. PLT014
(Refer to figure 21, 29)
(Area 3) The VOR is tuned to Elizabeth City VOR, and the aircraft is positioned over Shawboro. Which VOR indication is correct?

A — 2.
B — 5.
C — 9.

562. PLT014
(Refer to figure 22)
What course should be selected on the omnibearing selector (OBS) to make a direct flight from Mercer County Regional Airport (area 3) to the Minot VORTAC (area 1) with a TO indication?

A — 359°.
B — 179°.
C — 001°.

563. PLT012
(Refer to figure 24)
What is the approximate position of the aircraft if the VOR receivers indicate the 320° radial of Savannah VORTAC (area 3) and the 184° radial of Allendale VOR (area 1)?

A — Town of Guyton.
B — Town of Springfield.
C — 3 miles east of Marlow.

564. PLT014
(Refer to figure 24)
On what course should the VOR receiver (OBS) be set to navigate direct from Hampton Varnville Airport (area 1) to Savannah VORTAC (area 3)?

A — 200°.
B — 183°.
C — 003°.

565. PLT014
(Refer to figure 25)
What is the approximate position of the aircraft if the VOR receivers indicate the 245° radial of Sulphur Springs VOR-DME (area 5) and the 140° radial of Bonham VORTAC (area 3)?

A — Meadowview Airport.
B — Glenmar Airport.
C — Majors Airport.

566. PLT014
(Refer to figure 25)
On what course should the VOR receiver (OBS) be set in order to navigate direct from Majors Airport (area 1) to Quitman VORTAC (area 2)?

A — 101°.
B — 108°.
C — 281°.

567. PLT014
(Refer to figure 25, 29)
The VOR is tuned to Bonham VORTAC (area 3), and the aircraft is positioned over the town of Sulphur Springs (area 5). Which VOR indication is correct?

A — 1
B — 7
C — 8

568. PLT014

(Refer to figure 26)
(Area 5) The VOR is tuned to the Dallas/Fort Worth VORTAC. The omnibearing selector (OBS) is set on 253°, with a TO indication, and a right course deviation indicator (CDI) deflection. What is the aircraft's position from the VORTAC?

A — East-northeast.
B — North-northeast.
C — West-southwest.

569. PLT014

(Refer to figure 27, 29)
(Areas 4 and 3). The VOR is tuned to Jamestown VOR, and the aircraft is positioned over Cooperstown Airport. Which VOR indication is correct?

A — 1
B — 4
C — 6

570. PLT014

(Refer to figure 29)
(Illustration 1) The VOR receiver has the indications shown. What is the aircraft's position relative to the station?

A — North.
B — East.
C — South.

571. PLT014

(Refer to figure 29)
(Illustration 3) The VOR receiver has the indications shown. What is the aircraft's position relative to the station?

A — East.
B — Southeast.
C — West.

572. PLT014

(Refer to figure 29)
(Illustration 8) The VOR receiver has the indications shown. What radial is the aircraft crossing?

A — 030°.
B — 210°.
C — 300°.

573. PLT014

When the course deviation indicator (CDI) needle is centered during an omnireceiver check using a VOR test signal (VOT), the omnibearing selector (OBS) and the TO/FROM indicator should read

A — 180° FROM, only if the pilot is due north of the VOT.
B — 0° TO or 180° FROM, regardless of the pilot's position from the VOT.
C — 0° FROM or 180° TO, regardless of the pilot's position from the VOT.

574. PLT014

(Refer to figure 30)
(Illustration 1) Determine the magnetic bearing TO the station.

A — 030°.
B — 180°.
C — 210°.

575. PLT014

(Refer to figure 30)
(Illustration 2) What magnetic bearing should the pilot use to fly TO the station?

A — 010°.
B — 145°.
C — 190°.

576. PLT014

(Refer to figure 30)
(Illustration 2) Determine the approximate heading to intercept the 180° bearing TO the station.

A — 040°.
B — 160°.
C — 220°.

577. PLT014

(Refer to figure 30)
(Illustration 3) What is the magnetic bearing FROM the station?

A — 025°.
B — 115°.
C — 295°.

578. PLT014
(Refer to figure 30)
Which ADF indication represents the aircraft tracking TO the station with a right crosswind?

A — 1.
B — 2.
C — 4.

579. PLT014
(Refer to figure 30)
(Illustration 1) What outbound bearing is the aircraft crossing?

A — 030°.
B — 150°.
C — 180°.

580. PLT014
(Refer to figure 31)
(Illustration 1) The relative bearing TO the station is

A — 045°.
B — 180°.
C — 315°.

581. PLT014
(Refer to figure 31)
(Illustration 4) On a magnetic heading of 320°, the magnetic bearing TO the station is

A — 005°.
B — 185°.
C — 225°.

582. PLT014
(Refer to figure 31)
(Illustration 5) On a magnetic heading of 035°, the magnetic bearing TO the station is

A — 035°.
B — 180°.
C — 215°.

583. PLT014
(Refer to figure 31)
(Illustration 6) On a magnetic heading of 120°, the magnetic bearing TO the station is

A — 045°.
B — 165°.
C — 270°.

584. PLT014
(Refer to figure 31)
(Illustration 6) If the magnetic bearing TO the station is 240°, the magnetic heading is

A — 045°.
B — 105°.
C — 195°.

585. PLT014
(Refer to figure 31)
(Illustration 7) If the magnetic bearing TO the station is 030°, the magnetic heading is

A — 060°.
B — 120°.
C — 270°.

586. PLT014
(Refer to figure 31)
(Illustration 8) If the magnetic bearing TO the station is 135°, the magnetic heading is

A — 135°.
B — 270°.
C — 360°.

587. PLT354
How many satellites make up the Global Positioning System (GPS)?

A — 25.
B — 24.
C — 22.

588.   PLT354
How many Global Positioning System (GPS) satellites are required to yield a three dimensional position (latitude, longitude, and altitude) and time solution?

A — 5.
B — 4.
C — 6.

589.   PLT099
What is the most effective way to use the eyes during night flight?

A — Look only at far away, dim lights.
B — Scan slowly to permit offcenter viewing.
C — Concentrate directly on each object for a few seconds.

590.   PLT099
The best method to use when looking for other traffic at night is to

A — look to the side of the object and scan slowly.
B — scan the visual field very rapidly.
C — look to the side of the object and scan rapidly.

591.   PLT099
The most effective method of scanning for other aircraft for collision avoidance during nighttime hours is to use

A — regularly spaced concentration on the 3-, 9-, and 12-o'clock positions.
B — a series of short, regularly spaced eye movements to search each 30-degree sector.
C — peripheral vision by scanning small sectors and utilizing offcenter viewing.

592.   PLT333
During a night flight, you observe a steady red light and a flashing red light ahead and at the same altitude. What is the general direction of movement of the other aircraft?

A — The other aircraft is crossing to the left.
B — The other aircraft is crossing to the right.
C — The other aircraft is approaching head-on.

593.   PLT119
During a night flight, you observe a steady white light and a flashing red light ahead and at the same altitude. What is the general direction of movement of the other aircraft?

A — The other aircraft is flying away from you.
B — The other aircraft is crossing to the left.
C — The other aircraft is crossing to the right.

594.   PLT119
During a night flight, you observe steady red and green lights ahead and at the same altitude. What is the general direction of movement of the other aircraft?

A — The other aircraft is crossing to the left.
B — The other aircraft is flying away from you.
C — The other aircraft is approaching head-on.

595.   PLT333
VFR approaches to land at night should be accomplished

A — at a higher airspeed.
B — with a steeper descent.
C — the same as during daytime.

596.   PLT330
Large accumulations of carbon monoxide in the human body result in

A — tightness across the forehead.
B — loss of muscular power.
C — an increased sense of well-being.

597.   PLT330
Which statement best defines hypoxia?

A — A state of oxygen deficiency in the body.
B — An abnormal increase in the volume of air breathed.
C — A condition of gas bubble formation around the joints or muscles.

598. PLT332
When a stressful situation is encountered in flight, an abnormal increase in the volume of air breathed in and out can cause a condition known as

A — hyperventilation.
B — aerosinusitis.
C — aerotitis.

599. PLT332
Which would most likely result in hyperventilation?

A — Emotional tension, anxiety, or fear.
B — The excessive consumption of alcohol.
C — An extremely slow rate of breathing and insufficient oxygen.

600. PLT332
A pilot should be able to overcome the symptoms or avoid future occurrences of hyperventilation by

A — closely monitoring the flight instruments to control the airplane.
B — slowing the breathing rate, breathing into a bag, or talking aloud.
C — increasing the breathing rate in order to increase lung ventilation.

601. PLT097
Susceptibility to carbon monoxide poisoning increases as

A — altitude increases.
B — altitude decreases.
C — air pressure increases.

602. PLT333
What preparation should a pilot make to adapt the eyes for night flying?

A — Wear sunglasses after sunset until ready for flight.
B — Avoid red lights at least 30 minutes before the flight.
C — Avoid bright white lights at least 30 minutes before the flight.

603. PLT334
The danger of spatial disorientation during flight in poor visual conditions may be reduced by

A — shifting the eyes quickly between the exterior visual field and the instrument panel.
B — having faith in the instruments rather than taking a chance on the sensory organs.
C — leaning the body in the opposite direction of the motion of the aircraft.

604. PLT334
A state of temporary confusion resulting from misleading information being sent to the brain by various sensory organs is defined as

A — spatial disorientation.
B — hyperventilation.
C — hypoxia.

605. PLT334
Pilots are more subject to spatial disorientation if

A — they ignore the sensations of muscles and inner ear.
B — visual cues are taken away, as they are in instrument meteorological conditions (IMC).
C — eyes are moved often in the process of cross-checking the flight instruments.

606. PLT334
If a pilot experiences spatial disorientation during flight in a restricted visibility condition, the best way to overcome the effect is to

A — rely upon the aircraft instrument indications.
B — concentrate on yaw, pitch, and roll sensations.
C — consciously slow the breathing rate until symptoms clear and then resume normal breathing rate.

607. PLT103
What is it often called when a pilot pushes his or her capabilities and the aircraft's limits by trying to maintain visual contact with the terrain in low visibility and ceiling?

A — Scud running.
B — Mind set.
C — Peer pressure.

608. PLT104
What is the antidote when a pilot has a hazardous attitude, such as "Antiauthority"?

A — Rules do not apply in this situation.
B — I know what I am doing.
C — Follow the rules.

609. PLT104
What is the antidote when a pilot has a hazardous attitude, such as "Impulsivity"?

A — It could happen to me.
B — Do it quickly to get it over with.
C — Not so fast, think first.

610. PLT104
What is the antidote when a pilot has a hazardous attitude, such as "Invulnerability"?

A — It will not happen to me.
B — It cannot be that bad.
C — It could happen to me.

611. PLT104
What is the antidote when a pilot has a hazardous attitude, such as "Macho"?

A — I can do it.
B — Taking chances is foolish.
C — Nothing will happen.

612. PLT104
What is the antidote when a pilot has a hazardous attitude, such as "Resignation"?

A — What is the use.
B — Someone else is responsible.
C — I am not helpless.

613. PLT104
Who is responsible for determining whether a pilot is fit to fly for a particular flight, even though he or she holds a current medical certificate?

A — The FAA.
B — The medical examiner.
C — The pilot.

614. PLT104
What is the one common factor which affects most preventable accidents?

A — Structural failure.
B — Mechanical malfunction.
C — Human error.

615. PLT103
What often leads to spatial disorientation or collision with ground/obstacles when flying under Visual Flight Rules (VFR)?

A — Continual flight into instrument conditions.
B — Getting behind the aircraft.
C — Duck-under syndrome.

616. PLT104
What is one of the neglected items when a pilot relies on short and long term memory for repetitive tasks?

A — Checklists.
B — Situation awareness.
C — Flying outside the envelope.

617. PLT103
Hazardous attitudes occur to every pilot to some degree at some time. What are some of these hazardous attitudes?

A — Poor risk management and lack of stress management.
B — Antiauthority, impulsivity, macho, resignation, and invulnerability.
C — Poor situational awareness, snap judgments, and lack of a decision making process.

618. PLT103
In the aeronautical decision making (ADM) process, what is the first step in neutralizing a hazardous attitude?

A — Making a rational judgment.
B — Recognizing hazardous thoughts.
C — Recognizing the invulnerability of the situation.

619. PLT104
Risk management, as part of the aeronautical decision making (ADM) process, relies on which features to reduce the risks associated with each flight?

A — Application of stress management and risk element procedures.
B — Situational awareness, problem recognition, and good judgment.
C — The mental process of analyzing all information in a particular situation and making a timely decision on what action to take.

620. PLT377
How long does the Airworthiness Certificate of an aircraft remain valid?

A — As long as the aircraft has a current Registration Certificate.
B — Indefinitely, unless the aircraft suffers major damage.
C — As long as the aircraft is maintained and operated as required by Federal Aviation Regulations.

621. PLT444
During the preflight inspection who is responsible for determining the aircraft is safe for flight?

A — The owner or operator.
B — The certificated mechanic who performed the annual inspection.
C — The pilot in command.

622. PLT444
How should an aircraft preflight inspection be accomplished for the first flight of the day?

A — Thorough and systematic means recommended by the manufacturer.
B — Quick walk around with a check of gas and oil.
C — Any sequence as determined by the pilot-in-command.

623. PLT377
Who is primarily responsible for maintaining an aircraft in airworthy condition?

A — Pilot-in-command.
B — Owner or operator.
C — Mechanic.

624. PLT383
The definition of nighttime is

A — sunset to sunrise.
B — 1 hour after sunset to 1 hour before sunrise.
C — the time between the end of evening civil twilight and the beginning of morning civil twilight.

625. PLT506
Which V-speed represents maximum flap extended speed?

A — V_{FE}
B — V_{LOF}
C — V_{FC}

626. PLT506
Which V-speed represents maximum landing gear extended speed?

A — V_{LE}
B — V_{LO}
C — V_{FE}

627. PLT506
V_{NO} is defined as the

A — normal operating range.
B — never-exceed speed.
C — maximum structural cruising speed.

628. PLT506
V$_{SO}$ is defined as the

A — stalling speed or minimum steady flight speed in the landing configuration.
B — stalling speed or minimum steady flight speed in a specified configuration.
C — stalling speed or minimum takeoff safety speed.

629. PLT446
Which operation would be described as preventive maintenance?

A — Repair of landing gear brace struts.
B — Replenishing hydraulic fluid.
C — Repair of portions of skin sheets by making additional seams.

630. PLT446
Which operation would be described as preventive maintenance?

A — Repair of landing gear brace struts.
B — Replenishing hydraulic fluid.
C — Repair of portions of skin sheets by making additional seams.

631. PLT399
What document(s) must be in your personal possession or readily accessible in the aircraft while operating as pilot in command of an aircraft?

A — A pilot certificate with an endorsement showing accomplishment of an annual flight review and a pilot logbook showing recency of experience.
B — Certificates showing accomplishment of a checkout in the aircraft and a current biennial flight review.
C — An appropriate pilot certificate and an appropriate current medical certificate if required.

632. PLT399
When must a current pilot certificate be in the pilot's personal possession or readily accessible in the aircraft?

A — When acting as a crew chief during launch and recovery.
B — Only when passengers are carried.
C — Anytime when acting as pilot in command or as a required crewmember.

633. PLT399
A recreational or private pilot acting as pilot in command, or in any other capacity as a required pilot flight crewmember, must have in his or her personal possession or readily accessible in the aircraft a current

A — endorsement on the pilot certificate to show that a flight review has been satisfactorily accomplished.
B — medical certificate if required and an appropriate pilot certificate.
C — logbook endorsement to show that a flight review has been satisfactorily accomplished.

634. PLT399
Each person who holds a pilot certificate or a medical certificate shall present it for inspection upon the request of the Administrator, the National Transportation Safety Board, or any

A — authorized representative of the Department of Transportation.
B — person in a position of authority.
C — Federal, state, or local law enforcement officer.

635. PLT427
A Third-Class Medical Certificate is issued to a 36-year-old pilot on August 10, this year. To exercise the privileges of a Private Pilot Certificate, the medical certificate will be valid until midnight on

A — August 10, 3 years later.
B — August 31, 3 years later.
C — August 31, 5 years later.

636. PLT427
A Third-Class Medical Certificate is issued to a 51-year-old pilot on May 3, this year. To exercise the privileges of a Private Pilot Certificate, the medical certificate will be valid until midnight on

A — May 3, 1 year later.
B — May 31, 1 year later.
C — May 31, 2 years later.

637. PLT427
For private pilot operations, a Second-Class Medical Certificate issued to a 42-year-old pilot on July 15, this year, will expire at midnight on

A — July 15, 2 years later.
B — July 31, 1 year later.
C — July 31, 2 years later.

638. PLT447
For private pilot operations, a First-Class Medical Certificate issued to a 23-year-old pilot on October 21, this year, will expire at midnight on

A — October 21, 2 years later.
B — October 31, next year.
C — October 31, 5 years later.

639. PLT399
The pilot in command is required to hold a type rating in which aircraft?

A — Aircraft involved in ferry flights, training flights, or test flights.
B — Aircraft having a gross weight of more than 12,500 pounds.
C — Aircraft operated under an authorization issued by the Administrator.

640. PLT399
What is the definition of a high-performance airplane?

A — An airplane with 180 horsepower, or retractable landing gear, flaps, and a fixed-pitch propeller.
B — An airplane with a normal cruise speed in excess of 200 knots.
C — An airplane with an engine of more than 200 horsepower.

641. PLT399
Before a person holding a private pilot certificate may act as pilot in command of a high-performance airplane, that person must have

A — passed a flight test in that airplane from an FAA inspector.
B — an endorsement in that person's logbook that he or she is competent to act as pilot in command.
C — received ground and flight instruction from an authorized flight instructor who then endorses that person's logbook.

642. PLT448
In order to act as pilot in command of a high-performance airplane, a pilot must have

A — received and logged ground and flight instruction in an airplane that has more than 200 horsepower.
B — made and logged three solo takeoffs and landings in a high-performance airplane.
C — passed a flight test in a high-performance airplane.

643. PLT444
To act as pilot in command of an aircraft carrying passengers, a pilot must show by logbook endorsement the satisfactory completion of a flight review or completion of a pilot proficiency check within the preceding

A — 6 calendar months.
B — 12 calendar months.
C — 24 calendar months.

644. PLT444
If recency of experience requirements for night flight are not met and official sunset is 1830, the latest time passengers may be carried is

A — 1829.
B — 1859.
C — 1929.

645. PLT444

To act as pilot in command of an aircraft carrying passengers, the pilot must have made at least three takeoffs and three landings in an aircraft of the same category, class, and if a type rating is required, of the same type, within the preceding

A — 90 days.
B — 12 calendar months.
C — 24 calendar months.

646. PLT444

To act as pilot in command of an aircraft carrying passengers, the pilot must have made three takeoffs and three landings within the preceding 90 days in an aircraft of the same

A — make and model.
B — category and class, but not type.
C — category, class, and type, if a type rating is required.

647. PLT451

The takeoffs and landings required to meet the recency of experience requirements for carrying passengers in a tailwheel airplane

A — may be touch and go or full stop.
B — must be touch and go.
C — must be to a full stop.

648. PLT451

The three takeoffs and landings that are required to act as pilot in command at night must be done during the time period from

A — sunset to sunrise.
B — 1 hour after sunset to 1 hour before sunrise.
C — the end of evening civil twilight to the beginning of morning civil twilight.

649. PLT444

To meet the recency of experience requirements to act as pilot in command carrying passengers at night, a pilot must have made at least three takeoffs and three landings to a full stop within the preceding 90 days in

A — the same category and class of aircraft to be used.
B — the same type of aircraft to be used.
C — any aircraft.

650. PLT387

If a certificated pilot changes permanent mailing address and fails to notify the FAA Airmen Certification Branch of the new address, the pilot is entitled to exercise the privileges of the pilot certificate for a period of only

A — 30 days after the date of the move.
B — 60 days after the date of the move.
C — 90 days after the date of the move.

651. PLT444

A certificated private pilot may not act as pilot in command of an aircraft towing a glider unless there is entered in the pilot's logbook a minimum of

A — 100 hours of pilot-in-command time in the aircraft category, class, and type, if required, that the pilot is using to tow a glider.
B — 200 hours of pilot-in-command time in the aircraft category, class, and type, if required, that the pilot is using to tow a glider.
C — 100 hours of pilot flight time in any aircraft, that the pilot is using to tow a glider.

652. PLT444

To act as pilot in command of an aircraft towing a glider, a pilot is required to have made within the preceding 12 months

A — at least three flights in a powered glider.
B — at least three flights as observer in a glider being towed by an aircraft.
C — at least three actual or simulated glider tows while accompanied by a qualified pilot.

653. PLT444

A recreational pilot acting as pilot in command must have in his or her personal possession while aboard the aircraft

A — a current logbook endorsement to show that a flight review has been satisfactorily accomplished.
B — the pilot logbook to show recent experience requirements to serve as pilot in command have been met.
C — a current logbook endorsement that permits flight within 50 nautical miles from the departure airport.

654. PLT427

A third-class medical certificate was issued to a 19-year-old pilot on August 10, this year. To exercise the privileges of a recreational or private pilot certificate, the medical certificate will expire at midnight on

A — August 31, 5 years later.
B — August 31, 2 years later.
C — August 10, 2 years later.

655. PLT407

If a recreational or private pilot had a flight review on August 8, this year, when is the next flight review required?

A — August 31, next year.
B — August 8, 2 years later.
C — August 31, 2 years later.

656. PLT407

Each recreational or private pilot is required to have

A — an annual flight review.
B — a biennial flight review.
C — a semiannual flight review.

657. PLT407

If a recreational or private pilot had a flight review on August 8, this year, when is the next flight review required?

A — August 31, 2 years later.
B — August 31, 1 year later.
C — August 8, next year.

658. PLT448

How many passengers is a recreational pilot allowed to carry on board?

A — One.
B — Two.
C — Three.

659. PLT448

According to regulations pertaining to privileges and limitations, a recreational pilot may

A — not be paid in any manner for the operating expenses of a flight.
B — be paid for the operating expenses of a flight.
C — not pay less than the pro rata share of the operating expenses of a flight with a passenger.

660. PLT448

In regard to privileges and limitations, a recreational pilot may

A — not pay less than the pro rata share of the operating expenses of a flight with a passenger.
B — fly for compensation or hire within 50 nautical miles from the departure airport with a logbook endorsement.
C — not be paid in any manner for the operating expenses of a flight from a passenger.

661. PLT448

When may a recreational pilot act as pilot in command on a cross-country flight that exceeds 50 nautical miles from the departure airport?

A — After receiving ground and flight instructions on cross-country training and a logbook endorsement.
B — After attaining 100 hours of pilot-in-command time and a logbook endorsement.
C — 12 calendar months after receiving his or her recreational pilot certificate and a logbook endorsement.

662. PLT448
A recreational pilot may act as pilot in command of an aircraft that is certificated for a maximum of how many occupants?

A — Two.
B — Three.
C — Four.

663. PLT448
A recreational pilot may act as pilot in command of an aircraft with a maximum engine horsepower of

A — 160.
B — 180.
C — 200.

664. PLT448
What exception, if any, permits a recreational pilot to act as pilot in command of an aircraft carrying a passenger for hire?

A — If the passenger pays no more than the operating expenses.
B — If a donation is made to a charitable organization for the flight.
C — There is no exception.

665. PLT448
May a recreational pilot act as pilot in command of an aircraft in furtherance of a business?

A — Yes, if the flight is only incidental to that business.
B — Yes, providing the aircraft does not carry a person or property for compensation or hire.
C — No, it is not allowed.

666. PLT448
With respect to daylight hours, what is the earliest time a recreational pilot may take off?

A — One hour before sunrise.
B — At sunrise.
C — At the beginning of morning civil twilight.

667. PLT448
If sunset is 2021 and the end of evening civil twilight is 2043, when must a recreational pilot terminate the flight?

A — 2021.
B — 2043.
C — 2121.

668. PLT448
When may a recreational pilot operate to or from an airport that lies within Class C Airspace?

A — Anytime the control tower is in operation.
B — When the ceiling is at least 1,000 feet and the surface visibility is at least 2 miles.
C — For the purpose of obtaining an additional certificate or rating while under the supervision of an authorized flight instructor.

669. PLT448
Under what conditions may a recreational pilot operate at an airport that lies within Class D airspace and that has a part-time control tower in operation?

A — Any time when the tower is in operation, the ceiling is at least 3,000 feet, and the visibility is more than 1 mile.
B — Between sunrise and sunset when the tower is in operation, the ceiling is at least 2,500 feet, and the visibility is at least 3 miles.
C — Between sunrise and sunset when the tower is closed, the ceiling is at least 1,000 feet, and the visibility is at least 3 miles.

670. PLT448
When may a recreational pilot fly above 10,000 feet MSL?

A — When 2,000 feet AGL or below.
B — When 2,500 feet AGL or below.
C — When outside of controlled airspace.

671. PLT448
During daytime, what is the minimum flight or surface visibility required for recreational pilots in Class G airspace below 10,000 feet MSL?

A — 1 mile.
B — 3 miles.
C — 5 miles.

672. PLT448
During daytime, what is the minimum flight visibility required for recreational pilots in controlled airspace below 10,000 feet MSL?

A — 1 mile.
B — 3 miles.
C — 5 miles.

673. PLT448
Under what conditions, if any, may a recreational pilot demonstrate an aircraft in flight to a prospective buyer?

A — The buyer pays all the operating expenses.
B — The flight is not outside the United States.
C — None.

674. PLT448
When, if ever, may a recreational pilot act as pilot in command in an aircraft towing a banner?

A — If the pilot has logged 100 hours of flight time in powered aircraft.
B — If the pilot has an endorsement in his/her pilot logbook from an authorized flight instructor.
C — It is not allowed.

675. PLT448
When must a recreational pilot have a pilot-in-command flight check?

A — Every 400 hours.
B — Every 180 days.
C — If the pilot has less than 400 total flight hours and has not flown as pilot in command in an aircraft within the preceding 180 days.

676. PLT448
When may a recreational pilot act as pilot in command of an aircraft at night?

A — When obtaining an additional certificate or rating under the supervision of an authorized instructor, provided the surface or flight visibility is at least 1 statute mile.
B — When obtaining an additional certificate or rating under the supervision of an authorized instructor, provided the surface or flight visibility is at least 3 statute miles.
C — When obtaining an additional certificate or rating under the supervision of an authorized instructor, provided the surface or flight visibility is at least 5 statute miles.

677. PLT448
In regard to privileges and limitations, a private pilot may

A — not be paid in any manner for the operating expenses of a flight.
B — not pay less than the pro rata share of the operating expenses of a flight with passengers provided the expenses involve only fuel, oil, airport expenditures, or rental fees.
C — act as pilot in command of an aircraft carrying a passenger for compensation if the flight is in connection with a business or employment.

678. PLT448
According to regulations pertaining to privileges and limitations, a private pilot may

A — not pay less than the pro rata share of the operating expenses of a flight with passengers provided the expenses involve only fuel, oil, airport expenditures, or rental fees.
B — not be paid in any manner for the operating expenses of a flight.
C — be paid for the operating expenses of a flight if at least three takeoffs and three landings were made by the pilot within the preceding 90 days.

679. PLT448
What exception, if any, permits a private pilot to act as pilot in command of an aircraft carrying passengers who pay for the flight?

A — If the passengers pay all the operating expenses.
B — If a donation is made to a charitable organization for the flight.
C — There is no exception.

680. PLT378
What should an owner or operator know about Airworthiness Directives (ADs)?

A — For Informational purposes only.
B — They are mandatory.
C — They are voluntary.

681. PLT377
May a pilot operate an aircraft that is not in compliance with an Airworthiness Directive (AD)?

A — Yes, under VFR conditions only.
B — Yes, ADs are only voluntary.
C — Yes, if allowed by the AD.

682. PLT446
Preventive maintenance has been performed on an aircraft. What paperwork is required?

A — A full, detailed description of the work done must be entered in the airframe logbook.
B — The date the work was completed, and the name of the person who did the work must be entered in the airframe and engine logbook.
C — The signature, certificate number, and kind of certificate held by the person approving the work and a description of the work must be entered in the aircraft maintenance records.

683. PLT446
What regulation allows a private pilot to perform preventive maintenance?

A — 14 CFR Part 43.7.
B — 14 CFR Part 91.403.
C — 14 CFR Part 61.113.

684. PLT446
Who may perform preventive maintenance on an aircraft and approve it for return to service?

A — Student or Recreational pilot.
B — Private or Commercial pilot.
C — None of the above.

685. PLT444
The final authority as to the operation of an aircraft is the

A — Federal Aviation Administration.
B — pilot in command.
C — aircraft manufacturer.

686. PLT444
The person directly responsible for the pre-launch briefing of passengers for a flight is the

A — safety officer.
B — pilot in command.
C — ground crewmember.

687. PLT444
If an in-flight emergency requires immediate action, the pilot in command may

A — deviate from the FAR's to the extent required to meet the emergency, but must submit a written report to the Administrator within 24 hours.
B — deviate from the FAR's to the extent required to meet that emergency.
C — not deviate from the FAR's unless prior to the deviation approval is granted by the Administrator.

688. PLT444
When must a pilot who deviates from a regulation during an emergency send a written report of that deviation to the Administrator?

A — Within 7 days.
B — Within 10 days.
C — Upon request.

689. PLT444
Who is responsible for determining if an aircraft is in condition for safe flight?

A — A certificated aircraft mechanic.
B — The pilot in command.
C — The owner or operator.

690. PLT401
Under what conditions may objects be dropped from an aircraft?

A — Only in an emergency.
B — If precautions are taken to avoid injury or damage to persons or property on the surface.
C — If prior permission is received from the Federal Aviation Administration.

691. PLT463
A person may not act as a crewmember of a civil aircraft if alcoholic beverages have been consumed by that person within the preceding

A — 8 hours.
B — 12 hours.
C — 24 hours.

692. PLT463
Under what condition, if any, may a pilot allow a person who is obviously under the influence of drugs to be carried aboard an aircraft?

A — In an emergency or if the person is a medical patient under proper care.
B — Only if the person does not have access to the cockpit or pilot's compartment.
C — Under no condition.

693. PLT463
No person may attempt to act as a crewmember of a civil aircraft with

A — .008 percent by weight or more alcohol in the blood.
B — .004 percent by weight or more alcohol in the blood.
C — .04 percent by weight or more alcohol in the blood.

694. PLT440
Which preflight action is specifically required of the pilot prior to each flight?

A — Check the aircraft logbooks for appropriate entries.
B — Become familiar with all available information concerning the flight.
C — Review wake turbulence avoidance procedures.

695. PLT440
Preflight action, as required for all flights away from the vicinity of an airport, shall include

A — the designation of an alternate airport.
B — a study of arrival procedures at airports/heliports of intended use.
C — an alternate course of action if the flight cannot be completed as planned.

696. PLT440
In addition to other preflight actions for a VFR flight away from the vicinity of the departure airport, regulations specifically require the pilot in command to

A — review traffic control light signal procedures.
B — check the accuracy of the navigation equipment and the emergency locator transmitter (ELT).
C — determine runway lengths at airports of intended use and the aircraft's takeoff and landing distance data.

697. PLT465
Flight crewmembers are required to keep their safety belts and shoulder harnesses fastened during

A — takeoffs and landings.
B — all flight conditions.
C — flight in turbulent air.

698. PLT465
Which best describes the flight conditions under which flight crewmembers are specifically required to keep their safety belts and shoulder harnesses fastened?

A — Safety belts during takeoff and landing; shoulder harnesses during takeoff and landing.
B — Safety belts during takeoff and landing; shoulder harnesses during takeoff and landing and while en route.
C — Safety belts during takeoff and landing and while en route; shoulder harnesses during takeoff and landing.

699. PLT465
With respect to passengers, what obligation, if any, does a pilot in command have concerning the use of safety belts?

A — The pilot in command must instruct the passengers to keep safety belts fastened for the entire flight.
B — The pilot in command must brief the passengers on the use of safety belts and notify them to fasten their safety belts during taxi, takeoff, and landing.
C — The pilot in command has no obligation in regard to passengers' use of safety belts.

700. PLT465
With certain exceptions, safety belts are required to be secured about passengers during

A — taxi, takeoffs, and landings.
B — all flight conditions.
C — flight in turbulent air.

701. PLT465
Safety belts are required to be properly secured about which persons in an aircraft and when?

A — Pilots only, during takeoffs and landings.
B — Passengers, during taxi, takeoffs, and landings only.
C — Each person on board the aircraft during the entire flight.

702. PLT444
No person may operate an aircraft in formation flight

A — over a densely populated area.
B — in Class D Airspace under special VFR.
C — except by prior arrangement with the pilot in command of each aircraft.

703. PLT414
A seaplane and a motorboat are on crossing courses. If the motorboat is to the left of the seaplane, which has the right-of-way?

A — The motorboat.
B — The seaplane.
C — Both should alter course to the right.

704. PLT383
Unless otherwise authorized, what is the maximum indicated airspeed at which a person may operate an aircraft below 10,000 feet MSL?

A — 200 knots.
B — 250 knots.
C — 288 knots.

705. PLT161
Unless otherwise authorized, the maximum indicated airspeed at which aircraft may be flown when at or below 2,500 feet AGL and within 4 nautical miles of the primary airport of Class C airspace is

A — 200 knots.
B — 230 knots.
C — 250 knots.

706. PLT161
When flying in the airspace underlying Class B airspace, the maximum speed authorized is

A — 200 knots.
B — 230 knots.
C — 250 knots.

707. PLT161
When flying in a VFR corridor designated through Class B airspace the maximum speed authorized is

A — 180 knots.
B — 200 knots.
C — 250 knots.

708. PLT370
When an ATC clearance has been obtained, no pilot in command may deviate from that clearance, unless that pilot obtains an amended clearance. The one exception to this regulation is

A — when the clearance states "at pilot's discretion."
B — an emergency.
C — if the clearance contains a restriction.

709. PLT370
When would a pilot be required to submit a detailed report of an emergency which caused the pilot to deviate from an ATC clearance?

A — When requested by ATC.
B — Immediately.
C — Within 7 days.

710. PLT403
What action, if any, is appropriate if the pilot deviates from an ATC instruction during an emergency and is given priority?

A — Take no special action since you are pilot in command.
B — File a detailed report within 48 hours to the chief of the appropriate ATC facility, if requested.
C — File a report to the FAA Administrator, as soon as possible.

711. PLT435
Which is the correct traffic pattern departure procedure to use at a noncontrolled airport?

A — Depart in any direction consistent with safety, after crossing the airport boundary.
B — Make all turns to the left.
C — Comply with any FAA traffic pattern established for the airport.

712. PLT413
What is the specific fuel requirement for flight under VFR during daylight hours in an airplane?

A — Enough to complete the flight at normal cruising speed with adverse wind conditions.
B — Enough to fly to the first point of intended landing and to fly after that for 30 minutes at normal cruising speed.
C — Enough to fly to the first point of intended landing and to fly after that for 45 minutes at normal cruising speed.

713. PLT413
What is the specific fuel requirement for flight under VFR at night in an airplane?

A — Enough to complete the flight at normal cruising speed with adverse wind conditions.
B — Enough to fly to the first point of intended landing and to fly after that for 30 minutes at normal cruising speed.
C — Enough to fly to the first point of intended landing and to fly after that for 45 minutes at normal cruising speed.

714. PLT163
What minimum visibility and clearance from clouds are required for a recreational pilot in Class G airspace at 1,200 feet AGL or below during daylight hours?

A — 1 mile visibility and clear of clouds.
B — 3 miles visibility and clear of clouds.
C — 3 miles visibility, 500 feet below the clouds.

715. PLT163
Outside controlled airspace, the minimum flight visibility requirement for a recreational pilot flying VFR above 1,200 feet AGL and below 10,000 feet MSL during daylight hours is

A — 1 mile.
B — 3 miles.
C — 5 miles.

716. PLT400
In addition to a valid Airworthiness Certificate, what documents or records must be aboard an aircraft during flight?

A — Aircraft engine and airframe logbooks, and owner's manual.
B — Radio operator's permit, and repair and alteration forms.
C — Operating limitations and Registration Certificate.

717. PLT402
When must batteries in an emergency locator transmitter (ELT) be replaced or recharged, if rechargeable?

A — After any inadvertent activation of the ELT.
B — When the ELT has been in use for more than 1 cumulative hour.
C — When the ELT can no longer be heard over the airplane's communication radio receiver.

718. PLT402
When are non-rechargeable batteries of an emergency locator transmitter (ELT) required to be replaced?

A — Every 24 months.
B — When 50 percent of their useful life expires.
C — At the time of each 100-hour or annual inspection.

719. PLT461
Except in Alaska, during what time period should lighted position lights be displayed on an aircraft?

A — End of evening civil twilight to the beginning of morning civil twilight.
B — 1 hour after sunset to 1 hour before sunrise.
C — Sunset to sunrise.

720. PLT438
When operating an aircraft at cabin pressure altitudes above 12,500 feet MSL up to and including 14,000 feet MSL, supplemental oxygen shall be used during

A — the entire flight time at those altitudes.
B — that flight time in excess of 10 minutes at those altitudes.
C — that flight time in excess of 30 minutes at those altitudes.

721. PLT438
Unless each occupant is provided with supplemental oxygen, no person may operate a civil aircraft of U.S. registry above a maximum cabin pressure altitude of

A — 12,500 feet MSL.
B — 14,000 feet MSL.
C — 15,000 feet MSL.

722. PLT369
No person may operate an aircraft in acrobatic flight when

A — flight visibility is less than 5 miles.
B — over any congested area of a city, town, or settlement.
C — less than 2,500 feet AGL.

723. PLT369
In which class of airspace is acrobatic flight prohibited?

A — Class E airspace not designated for Federal Airways above 1,500 feet AGL.
B — Class E airspace below 1,500 feet AGL.
C — Class G airspace above 1,500 feet AGL.

724. PLT369
What is the lowest altitude permitted for acrobatic flight?

A — 1,000 feet AGL.
B — 1,500 feet AGL.
C — 2,000 feet AGL.

725. PLT369
No person may operate an aircraft in acrobatic flight when the flight visibility is less than

A — 3 miles.
B — 5 miles.
C — 7 miles.

726. PLT405
An approved parachute constructed of natural materials must have been packed by a certificated and appropriately rated parachute rigger within the preceding

A — 60 days.
B — 90 days.
C — 120 days.

727. PLT405
An approved synthetic parachute may be carried in an aircraft for emergency use if it has been packed by an appropriately rated parachute rigger within the preceding

A — 120 days.
B — 180 days.
C — 365 days.

728. PLT405
With certain exceptions, when must each occupant of an aircraft wear an approved parachute?

A — When a door is removed from the aircraft to facilitate parachute jumpers.
B — When intentionally pitching the nose of the aircraft up or down 30° or more.
C — When intentionally banking in excess of 30°.

729. PLT373
Which is normally prohibited when operating a restricted category civil aircraft?

A — Flight under instrument flight rules.
B — Flight over a densely populated area.
C — Flight within Class D airspace.

730. PLT373
Unless otherwise specifically authorized, no person may operate an aircraft that has an experimental certificate

A — beneath the floor of Class B airspace.
B — over a densely populated area or in a congested airway.
C — from the primary airport within Class D airspace.

731. PLT374
The responsibility for ensuring that an aircraft is maintained in an airworthy condition is primarily that of the

A — pilot in command.
B — owner or operator.
C — mechanic who performs the work.

732. PLT377
The airworthiness of an aircraft can be determined by a preflight inspection and a

A — statement from the owner or operator that the aircraft is airworthy.
B — log book endorsement from a flight instructor.
C — review of the maintenance records.

733. PLT426
The responsibility for ensuring that maintenance personnel make the appropriate entries in the aircraft maintenance records indicating the aircraft has been approved for return to service lies with the

A — owner or operator.
B — pilot in command.
C — mechanic who performed the work.

734. PLT374
Who is responsible for ensuring appropriate entries are made in maintenance records indicating the aircraft has been approved for return to service?

A — Repair station.
B — Certified mechanic.
C — Owner or operator.

735. PLT374
Who is responsible for ensuring Airworthiness Directives (ADs) are complied with?

A — Mechanic with inspection authorization (IA).
B — Owner or operator.
C — Repair station.

736. PLT375
Completion of an annual inspection and the return of the aircraft to service should always be indicated by

A — the relicensing date on the Registration Certificate.
B — an appropriate notation in the aircraft maintenance records.
C — an inspection sticker placed on the instrument panel that lists the annual inspection completion date.

737. PLT375
If an alteration or repair substantially affects an aircraft's operation in flight, that aircraft must be test flown by an appropriately-rated pilot and approved for return to service prior to being operated

A — by any private pilot.
B — with passengers aboard.
C — for compensation or hire.

738. PLT375
Before passengers can be carried in an aircraft that has been altered in a manner that may have appreciably changed its flight characteristics, it must be flight tested by an appropriately rated pilot who holds at least a

A — Commercial Pilot Certificate with an instrument rating.
B — Private Pilot Certificate.
C — Commercial Pilot Certificate and a mechanic's certificate.

739. PLT372
An aircraft's annual inspection was performed on July 12, this year. The next annual inspection will be due no later than

A — July 1, next year.
B — July 13, next year.
C — July 31, next year.

740. PLT372
To determine the expiration date of the last annual aircraft inspection, a person should refer to the

A — Airworthiness Certificate.
B — Registration Certificate.
C — aircraft maintenance records.

741. PLT372
What aircraft inspections are required for rental aircraft that are also used for flight instruction?

A — Annual and 100-hour inspections.
B — Biannual and 100-hour inspections.
C — Annual and 50-hour inspections.

742. PLT372
An aircraft had a 100-hour inspection when the tachometer read 1259.6. When is the next 100-hour inspection due?

A — 1349.6 hours.
B — 1359.6 hours.
C — 1369.6 hours.

743. PLT372
A 100-hour inspection was due at 3302.5 hours on the tachometer. The 100-hour inspection was actually done at 3309.5 hours. When is the next 100-hour inspection due?

A — 3312.5 hours.
B — 3402.5 hours.
C — 3409.5 hours.

744. PLT372
Maintenance records show the last transponder inspection was performed on September 1, 2006. The next inspection will be due no later than

A — September 1, 2008.
B — September 30, 2007.
C — September 30, 2008.

745. PLT374
Which records or documents shall the owner or operator of an aircraft keep to show compliance with an applicable Airworthiness Directive?

A — Aircraft maintenance records.
B — Airworthiness Certificate and Pilot's Operating Handbook.
C — Airworthiness and Registration Certificates.

746. PLT161
All operations within Class C airspace must be in

A — accordance with instrument flight rules.
B — compliance with ATC clearances and instructions.
C — an aircraft equipped with a 4096-code transponder with Mode C encoding capability.

747. PLT366
If an aircraft is involved in an accident which results in substantial damage to the aircraft, the nearest NTSB field office should be notified

A — immediately.
B — within 48 hours.
C — within 7 days.

748. PLT366
Which incident requires an immediate notification to the nearest NTSB field office?

A — A forced landing due to engine failure.
B — Landing gear damage, due to a hard landing.
C — Flight control system malfunction or failure.

749. PLT366
Which incident would necessitate an immediate notification to the nearest NTSB field office?

A — An in-flight generator/alternator failure.
B — An in-flight fire.
C — An in-flight loss of VOR receiver capability.

750. PLT366
Which incident requires an immediate notification be made to the nearest NTSB field office?

A — An overdue aircraft that is believed to be involved in an accident.
B — An in-flight radio communications failure.
C — An in-flight generator or alternator failure.

751. PLT366
May aircraft wreckage be moved prior to the time the NTSB takes custody?

A — Yes, but only if moved by a federal, state, or local law enforcement officer.
B — Yes, but only to protect the wreckage from further damage.
C — No, it may not be moved under any circumstances.

752. PLT366
The operator of an aircraft that has been involved in an accident is required to file an accident report within how many days?

A — 5.
B — 7.
C — 10.

753. PLT366
The operator of an aircraft that has been involved in an incident is required to submit a report to the nearest field office of the NTSB

A — within 7 days.
B — within 10 days.
C — when requested.

754. PLT413
No person may begin a flight in a rotorcraft under VFR unless there is enough fuel to fly to the first point of intended landing and, assuming normal cruising speed, to fly thereafter for at least

A — 20 minutes.
B — 30 minutes.
C — 1 hour.

755. PLT161
Under what conditions, if any, may a private pilot operate a helicopter under special VFR at night within Class D airspace?

A — The helicopter must be fully instrument equipped and the pilot must be instrument rated.
B — The flight visibility must be at least 1 mile.
C — There are no conditions; regulations permit this.

756. PLT146
Which is appropriate for a helicopter approaching an airport for landing?

A — Remain below the airplane traffic pattern altitude.
B — Avoid the flow of fixed-wing traffic.
C — Fly right-hand traffic.

757. PLT092
(Refer to figure 43A, 43B)
What effect does adding a 185-pound passenger have on the CG, if prior to boarding the passenger, the helicopter weighed 1,380 pounds and the moment is 136,647.5 pound-inches?

A — The CG is moved forward 1.78 inches.
B — The CG is moved aft 1.78 inches.
C — The CG is moved forward 2.36 inches.

758. PLT264
If the pilot were to make a near-vertical power approach into a confined area with the airspeed near zero, what hazardous condition may develop?

A — Ground resonance when ground contact is made.
B — A settling-with-power condition.
C — Blade stall vibration could develop.

759. PLT268
With calm wind conditions, which flight operation would require the most power?

A — A right-hovering turn.
B — A left-hovering turn.
C — Hovering out of ground effect.

760. PLT285
(Refer to figure 47)
What is the best rate-of-climb speed for the helicopter?

A — 24 MPH.
B — 40 MPH.
C — 57 MPH.

761. PLT092
(Refer to figure 44)
Determine if the helicopter weight and balance is within limits.

    Empty weight...1,495.0 lbs.
        arm...101.4 in.
        moment/100...1,515.93
    Oil...8 qts.
        arm...100.5 inches
    Fuel...40 gal.
        arm...96.0 inches
    Pilot and copilot...300 lbs.
        arm...64 inches

A — CG 95.2 inches, within limits.
B — CG 95.3 inches, weight and CG out of limits.
C — CG 95.4 inches, within limits.

762. PLT021
(Refer to figure 44)
Calculate the weight and balance of the helicopter, and determine if the CG is within limits.

    Empty weight...1,495.0 lbs.
        arm...101.4 inches
        moment/100...1,515.93 lb.inches
    Oil...8 qts.
        arm...100.5 inches
    Fuel...40 gal.
        arm...96.0 inches
    Pilot...160.0 lbs.
        arm....64.0 inches

A — CG 90.48 inches, out of limits forward.
B — CG 95.32 inches, within limits.
C — CG 97.58 inches, within limits.

763. PLT285
(Refer to figure 47)
The airspeed range to avoid while flying in ground effect is

A — 25 - 40 MPH
B — 25 - 57 MPH
C — 40 MPH and above.

764. PLT092
How is the CG of the helicopter affected after a fuel burn of 20 gallons (arm 96.9)?

Gross weight prior to fuel burn...2,050 lbs.
Moment...195,365 lb-in.

A — CG shifts forward 1.0 inch.
B — CG shifts forward 0.1 inch.
C — CG shifts aft 1.0 inch.

765. PLT092
(Refer to figure 43A, 43B)
Determine if the helicopter's CG is within limits.

Empty weight (including oil)...1,025 lbs.
Moment...102,705 lb.inches
Pilot and passenger...345 lbs.
Fuel...35 gal.

A — Out of limits forward.
B — Within limits.
C — Out of limits aft.

766. PLT435
Select the UNICOM frequencies normally assigned to stations at landing areas used exclusively as heliports.

A — 122.75 and 123.65 MHz.
B — 123.0 and 122.95 MHz.
C — 123.05 and 123.075 MHz.

767. PLT092
(Refer to figure 42)
Determine the weight and balance of the helicopter.

Empty weight...1,495.0 lbs.
moment...151,593.0 lb-inches
Pilot and one passenger...350.0 lbs.
arm...64.0 inches
Fuel...(40 gal usable)
arm...96.0 inches

A — Over gross weight limit, but within CG limit.
B — Within gross weight limit and at the aft CG limit.
C — Over gross weight limit and exceeds the aft CG limit.

768. PLT092
(Refer to figure 44)
What action, if any, should be taken for lateral balance if the helicopter is loaded as follows?

Gross weight...1,800 lbs.
Pilot...140 lb, 13.5 in. left of "0" MOM arm
Copilot...180 lb, 13.5 in. right of "0" MOM arm

A — Add 10 pounds of weight to the pilot's side.
B — Decrease the gross weight 50 pounds.
C — No action is required.

769. PLT092
(Refer to figure 43A, 43B)
How is the CG of the helicopter affected when all of the auxiliary fuel is burned off?

Gross weight prior to fuel burn...1,660 lb
Moment...159,898.5 lb-in.

A — CG moves aft 0.12 inch.
B — CG moves forward 0.78 inch.
C — CG moves forward 1.07 inches.

770. PLT349
If possible, when departing a confined area, what type of takeoff is preferred?

A — A normal takeoff from a hover.
B — A vertical takeoff.
C — A normal takeoff from the surface.

771. PLT092
(Refer to figure 44)
What action should be taken for lateral balance if the helicopter is loaded as follows?

Gross weight..................1,800 lb
Pilot.........100 lb, 13.5 in. left of "0" MOM arm
Copilot...200 lb, 13.5 in. right of "0" MOM arm

A — Add 50 pounds of weight to the pilot's side.
B — Decrease the gross weight 50 pounds.
C — No action is required.

772. PLT285
(Refer to figure 47)
Which airspeed/altitude combination should be avoided during helicopter operations?

A — 30 MPH/200 feet AGL.
B — 50 MPH/300 feet AGL.
C — 60 MPH/20 feet AGL.

773. PLT221
Before beginning a confined area or pinnacle landing, the pilot should first

A — execute a high reconnaissance.
B — execute a low reconnaissance.
C — fly around the area to discover areas of turbulence.

774. PLT522
Which is a correct general rule for pinnacle and ridgeline operations?

A — Gaining altitude on takeoff is more important than gaining airspeed.
B — The approach path to a ridgeline is usually perpendicular to the ridge.
C — A climb to a pinnacle or ridgeline should be performed on the upwind side.

775. PLT349
Which action would be appropriate for confined area operations?

A — Takeoffs and landings must be made into the wind.
B — Plan the flightpath over areas suitable for a forced landing.
C — A very steep angle of descent should be used to land on the selected spot.

776. PLT521
Takeoff from a slope is normally accomplished by

A — moving the cyclic in a direction away from the slope.
B — bringing the helicopter to a level attitude before completely leaving the ground.
C — moving the cyclic stick to a full up position as the helicopter nears a level attitude.

777. PLT521
What is the procedure for a slope landing?

A — When the downslope skid is on the ground, hold the collective pitch at the same position.
B — Minimum RPM shall be held until the full weight of the helicopter is on the skid.
C — When parallel to the slope, slowly lower the upslope skid to the ground prior to lowering the downslope skid.

778. PLT169
If anti-torque failure occurred during the landing touchdown, what could be done to help straighten out a left yaw prior to touchdown?

A — A flare to zero airspeed and a vertical descent to touchdown should be made.
B — Apply available throttle to help swing the nose to the right just prior to touchdown.
C — A normal running landing should be made.

779. PLT175
Which is a precaution to be observed during an autorotative descent?

A — Normally, the airspeed is controlled with the collective pitch.
B — Normally, only the cyclic control is used to make turns.
C — Do not allow the rate of descent to get too low at zero airspeed.

780. PLT175
What action should the pilot take if engine failure occurs at altitude?

A — Open the throttle as the collective pitch is raised
B — Reduce cyclic back stick pressure during turns.
C — Lower the collective pitch control, as necessary, to maintain rotor RPM.

781. PLT222
Under what condition should a helicopter pilot consider using a running takeoff?

A — When gross weight or density altitude prevents a sustained hover at normal hovering altitude.
B — When a normal climb speed is assured between 10 and 20 feet.
C — When the additional airspeed can be quickly converted to altitude.

782. PLT486
Which flight technique is recommended for use during hot weather?

A — Use minimum allowable RPM and maximum allowable manifold pressure during all phases of flight.
B — During hovering flight, maintain minimum engine RPM during left pedal turns, and maximum engine RPM during right pedal turns.
C — During takeoff, accelerate slowly into forward flight.

783. PLT217
The proper action to initiate a quick stop is to apply

A — forward cyclic and lower the collective pitch.
B — aft cyclic and raise the collective pitch.
C — aft cyclic and lower the collective pitch.

784. PLT141
A lighted heliport may be identified by a

A — green, yellow, and white rotating beacon.
B — flashing yellow light.
C — blue lighted square landing area.

785. PLT285
(Refer to figure 47)
Which airspeed/altitude combination should be avoided during helicopter operations?

A — 20 MPH/200 feet AGL.
B — 35 MPH/175 feet AGL.
C — 40 MPH/75 feet AGL.

786. PLT131
Which is a result of the phenomenon of ground effect?

A — The induced angle of attack of each rotor blade is increased.
B — The lift vector becomes more horizontal.
C — The angle of attack generating lift is increased.

787. PLT235
During a hover, a helicopter tends to drift to the right. To compensate for this, some helicopters have the

A — tail rotor tilted to the left.
B — tail rotor tilted to the right.
C — rotor mast rigged to the left side.

788. PLT197
When a blade flaps up, the CG moves closer to its axis of rotation giving that blade a tendency to

A — decelerate.
B — accelerate.
C — stabilize its rotational velocity.

789. PLT027
The upward bending of the rotor blades resulting from the combined forces of lift and centrifugal force is known as

A — coning.
B — blade slapping.
C — inertia.

790. PLT168
Angle of attack is defined as the angle between the chord line of an airfoil and the

A — direction of the relative wind.
B — pitch angle of an airfoil.
C — rotor plane of rotation.

791. PLT235
Translational lift is the result of

A — decreased rotor efficiency.
B — airspeed.
C — both airspeed and groundspeed.

792. PLT472
While in level cruising flight in a helicopter, a pilot experiences low-frequency vibrations (100 to 400 cycles per minute). These vibrations are normally associated with the

A — engine.
B — cooling fan.
C — main rotor.

793. PLT235
The lift differential that exists between the advancing main rotor blade and the retreating main rotor blade is known as

A — transverse flow effect.
B — dissymmetry of lift.
C — hunting tendency.

794. PLT470
The primary purpose of the tail rotor system is to

A — assist in making a coordinated turn.
B — maintain heading during forward flight.
C — counteract the torque effect of the main rotor.

795. PLT112
If RPM is low and manifold pressure is high, what initial corrective action should be taken?

A — Increase the throttle.
B — Lower the collective pitch.
C — Raise the collective pitch.

796. PLT470
The purpose of the lead-lag (drag) hinge in a three-bladed, fully articulated helicopter rotor system is to compensate for

A — Coriolis effect.
B — coning.
C — geometric unbalance.

797. PLT235
High airspeeds, particularly in turbulent air, should be avoided primarily because of the possibility of

A — an abrupt pitchup.
B — retreating blade stall.
C — a low-frequency vibration developing.

798. PLT470
The maximum forward speed of a helicopter is limited by

A — retreating blade stall.
B — the rotor RPM red line.
C — solidity ratio.

799. PLT259
Ground resonance is most likely to develop when

A — on the ground and harmonic vibrations develop between the main and tail rotors.
B — a series of shocks causes the rotor system to become unbalanced.
C — there is a combination of a decrease in the angle of attack on the advancing blade and an increase in the angle of attack on the retreating blade.

800. PLT470
Select the helicopter component that, if defective, would cause medium-frequency vibrations.

A — Tail rotor.
B — Main rotor.
C — Engine.

801. PLT285
The Principal reason the shaded area of a Height vs. Velocity Chart should be avoided is

A — turbulence near the surface can dephase the blade dampers.
B — rotor RPM may decay before ground contact is made if an engine failure should occur.
C — insufficient airspeed would be available to ensure a safe landing in case of an engine failure.

802. PLT112
During surface taxiing, the collective pitch is used to control

A — drift during a crosswind.
B — rate of speed.
C — ground track.

803. PLT112

During surface taxiing, the cyclic pitch stick is used to control

A — forward movement.
B — heading.
C — ground track.

804. PLT235

When operating at high forward airspeeds, retreating blade stalls are more likely to occur under which condition?

A — Low gross weight and low density altitude.
B — High RPM and low density altitude.
C — Steep turns in turbulent air.

805. PLT265

If the pilot experiences ground resonance, and the rotor r.p.m. is not sufficient for flight,

A — open the throttle full and liftoff.
B — apply the rotor brake and stop the rotor as soon as possible.
C — attempt to takeoff at that power setting.

APPENDIX A

LEARNING STATEMENT CODES AND LEARNING STATEMENTS

To determine the knowledge area in which a particular question was incorrectly answered, compare the learning statement code(s) on the Federal Aviation Administration Airmen Computer Test Report to the following learning statement outline. The total number of test items missed may differ from the number of learning statement codes shown on the test report, since you may have missed more than one question in a specific learning statement code.

Learning Statement Codes and Learning Statements for Pilots, Instructors, Flight Engineers, Dispatchers, Navigators, and Pilot Examiners Exams

Code	Learning Statement
PLT001	Calculate a course intercept
PLT002	Calculate aircraft performance - airspeed
PLT003	Calculate aircraft performance - center of gravity
PLT004	Calculate aircraft performance - climb / descent
PLT005	Calculate aircraft performance - density altitude
PLT006	Calculate aircraft performance - glide
PLT007	Calculate aircraft performance - IAS / EPR
PLT008	Calculate aircraft performance - landing
PLT009	Calculate aircraft performance - measured gas temperature (MGT)
PLT010	Calculate aircraft performance - STAB TRIM
PLT011	Calculate aircraft performance - takeoff
PLT012	Calculate aircraft performance - time/speed/distance/course/fuel/wind
PLT013	Calculate crosswind / headwind components
PLT014	Calculate distance / bearing from/to a station
PLT015	Calculate flight performance / planning - range
PLT016	Calculate fuel dump - time / weight / volume
PLT017	Calculate L/D ratio
PLT018	Calculate load factor / stall speed / velocity / angle of attack
PLT019	Calculate pressure altitude
PLT020	Calculate turbulent air penetration
PLT021	Calculate weight and balance
PLT022	Define Aeronautical Decision Making (ADM)
PLT023	Define altitude - absolute / true / indicated / density / pressure
PLT024	Define atmospheric adiabatic process
PLT025	Define Bernoulli`s principle
PLT026	Define ceiling

Code	Learning Statement
PLT027	Define coning
PLT028	Define crewmember
PLT029	Define critical phase of flight
PLT030	Define false lift
PLT031	Define isobars / associated winds
PLT032	Define MACH speed regimes
PLT033	Define MEA / MOCA / MRA
PLT034	Define stopway / clearway
PLT035	Define Vne / Vno
PLT036	Interpret a MACH meter reading
PLT037	Interpret a radar weather report
PLT038	Interpret aircraft Power Schedule Chart
PLT039	Interpret airport landing indicator
PLT040	Interpret airspace classes - charts / diagrams
PLT041	Interpret altimeter - readings / settings
PLT042	Interpret Analysis Heights / Isotachs Chart
PLT043	Interpret Analysis Heights / Temperature Chart
PLT044	Interpret ATC communications / instructions / terminology
PLT045	Interpret Descent Performance Chart
PLT046	Interpret drag ratio from charts
PLT047	Interpret Flight Director - modes / operation / indications
PLT048	Interpret Hovering Ceiling Chart
PLT049	Interpret ILS - charts / RMI / CDI / indications
PLT050	Interpret information on a Brake Energy Limit Chart
PLT051	Interpret information on a Convective Outlook
PLT052	Interpret information on a Departure Procedure Chart
PLT053	Interpret information on a Flight Plan
PLT054	Interpret information on a Glider Performance Graph
PLT055	Interpret information on a High Altitude Chart
PLT056	Interpret information on a Horizontal Situation Indicator (HSI)
PLT057	Interpret information on a Hot Air Balloon Performance Graph
PLT058	Interpret information on a Low Altitude Chart
PLT059	Interpret information on a METAR / SPECI report
PLT060	Interpret information on a Performance Curve Chart
PLT061	Interpret information on a PIREP
PLT062	Interpret information on a Pseudo-Adiabatic Chart
PLT063	Interpret information on a Radar Summary Chart
PLT064	Interpret information on a Sectional Chart
PLT065	Interpret information on a Service Ceiling Engine Inoperative Chart
PLT066	Interpret information on a Severe Weather Outlook Chart
PLT067	Interpret information on a SIGMET
PLT068	Interpret information on a Significant Weather Prognostic Chart
PLT069	Interpret information on a Slush/Standing Water Takeoff chart
PLT070	Interpret information on a Stability Chart
PLT071	Interpret information on a Surface Analysis Chart

Code	Learning Statement
PLT072	Interpret information on a Terminal Aerodrome Forecast (TAF)
PLT073	Interpret information on a Tower Enroute Control (TEC)
PLT074	Interpret information on a Velocity/Load Factor Chart
PLT075	Interpret information on a Weather Depiction Chart
PLT076	Interpret information on a Winds and Temperatures Aloft Forecast (FD)
PLT077	Interpret information on an Airport Diagram
PLT078	Interpret information on an Airport Facility Directory (AFD)
PLT079	Interpret information on an Airways chart
PLT080	Interpret information on an Arrival Chart
PLT081	Interpret information on an Aviation Area Forecast (FA)
PLT082	Interpret information on an IFR Alternate Airport Minimums Chart
PLT083	Interpret information on an Instrument Approach Procedures (IAP)
PLT084	Interpret information on an Observed Winds Aloft Chart
PLT085	Interpret information on Takeoff Obstacle / Field / Climb Limit Charts
PLT086	Interpret readings on a Turn and Slip Indicator
PLT087	Interpret readings on an Aircraft Course and DME Indicator
PLT088	Interpret speed indicator readings
PLT089	Interpret Takeoff Speeds Chart
PLT090	Interpret VOR - charts / indications / CDI / ADF / NAV
PLT091	Interpret VOR / ADF / NDB / CDI / RMI - illustrations / indications / procedures
PLT092	Interpret weight and balance - diagram
PLT093	Recall administration of medical oxygen
PLT094	Recall aerodynamics - airfoil design / pressure distribution
PLT095	Recall aerodynamics - longitudinal axis / lateral axis
PLT096	Recall aeromedical factors - effects of altitude
PLT097	Recall aeromedical factors - effects of carbon monoxide poisoning
PLT098	Recall aeromedical factors - fitness for flight
PLT099	Recall aeromedical factors - scanning procedures
PLT100	Recall aeronautical charts - IFR En Route Low Altitude
PLT101	Recall aeronautical charts - pilotage
PLT102	Recall aeronautical charts - terminal procedures
PLT103	Recall Aeronautical Decision Making (ADM) - hazardous attitudes
PLT104	Recall Aeronautical Decision Making (ADM) - human factors
PLT105	Recall airborne radar / thunderstorm detection equipment - use / limitations
PLT106	Recall aircraft air-cycle machine
PLT107	Recall aircraft alternator / generator system
PLT108	Recall aircraft anti-icing / deicing - methods / fluids
PLT109	Recall aircraft batteries - capacity / charging / types / storage / rating / precautions
PLT110	Recall aircraft brake system
PLT111	Recall aircraft circuitry - series / parallel
PLT112	Recall aircraft controls - proper use / techniques
PLT113	Recall aircraft design - categories / limitation factors
PLT114	Recall aircraft design - construction / function
PLT115	Recall aircraft engine - detonation cause / characteristics
PLT116	Recall aircraft general knowledge / publications / AIM / navigational aids

Code	Learning Statement
PLT117	Recall aircraft heated windshields
PLT118	Recall aircraft instruments - gyroscopic
PLT119	Recall aircraft lighting - anti-collision / landing / navigation
PLT120	Recall aircraft limitations - turbulent air penetration
PLT121	Recall aircraft loading - computations
PLT122	Recall aircraft operations - checklist usage
PLT123	Recall aircraft performance - airspeed
PLT124	Recall aircraft performance - atmospheric effects
PLT125	Recall aircraft performance - climb / descent
PLT126	Recall aircraft performance - cold weather operations
PLT127	Recall aircraft performance - density altitude
PLT128	Recall aircraft performance - effects of icing
PLT129	Recall aircraft performance - effects of runway slope
PLT130	Recall aircraft performance - fuel
PLT131	Recall aircraft performance - ground effect
PLT132	Recall aircraft performance - instrument markings / airspeed / definitions / indications
PLT133	Recall aircraft performance - normal climb / descent rates
PLT134	Recall aircraft performance - takeoff
PLT135	Recall aircraft pressurization - system / operation
PLT136	Recall aircraft systems - anti-icing / deicing
PLT137	Recall aircraft systems - environmental control
PLT138	Recall aircraft tires - types / characteristics
PLT139	Recall aircraft warning systems - stall / fire / retractable gear / terrain awareness
PLT140	Recall airport operations - LAHSO
PLT141	Recall airport operations - markings / signs / lighting
PLT142	Recall airport operations - noise avoidance routes
PLT143	Recall airport operations - rescue / fire fighting vehicles and types of agents
PLT144	Recall airport operations - runway conditions
PLT145	Recall airport operations - runway lighting
PLT146	Recall airport operations - traffic pattern procedures
PLT147	Recall airport operations - visual glideslope indicators
PLT148	Recall airport operations lighting - MALS / ALSF / RCLS / TDZL
PLT149	Recall airport taxi operations - procedures
PLT150	Recall airport traffic patterns - entry procedures
PLT151	Recall airship - buoyancy
PLT152	Recall airship - flight characteristics / controllability
PLT153	Recall airship - flight operations
PLT154	Recall airship - ground weigh-off / static / trim condition
PLT155	Recall airship - maintaining pressure
PLT156	Recall airship - maximum headway / flight at equilibrium
PLT157	Recall airship - pressure height / dampers / position
PLT158	Recall airship - pressure height / manometers
PLT159	Recall airship - pressure height / super heat / valving gas
PLT160	Recall airship - stability / control / positive superheat
PLT161	Recall airspace classes - limits / requirements / restrictions / airspeeds / equipment

Code	Learning Statement
PLT162	Recall airspace requirements - operations
PLT163	Recall airspace requirements - visibility / cloud clearance
PLT163	Recall airspeed - effects during a turn
PLT164	Recall altimeter - effect of temperature changes
PLT165	Recall altimeter - settings / setting procedures
PLT167	Recall altimeters - characteristics / accuracy
PLT168	Recall angle of attack - characteristics / forces / principles
PLT169	Recall antitorque system - components / functions
PLT170	Recall approach / landing / taxiing techniques
PLT171	Recall ATC - reporting
PLT172	Recall ATC - system / services
PLT173	Recall atmospheric conditions - measurements / pressure / stability
PLT174	Recall autopilot - components / operating principles / characteristics
PLT175	Recall autorotation
PLT176	Recall balance tab - purpose / operation
PLT177	Recall balloon - flight operations
PLT178	Recall balloon - flight operations / gas
PLT179	Recall balloon - ground weigh-off / static equilibrium / load
PLT180	Recall balloon - hot air / lift / false lift / characteristics
PLT181	Recall balloon - hot air / physics
PLT182	Recall balloon - inspecting the fabric
PLT183	Recall balloon flight operations - ascent / descent
PLT184	Recall balloon flight operations - launch / landing
PLT185	Recall basic instrument flying - fundamental skills
PLT186	Recall basic instrument flying - pitch instruments
PLT187	Recall basic instrument flying - turn coordinator / turn and slip indicator
PLT188	Recall cabin atmosphere control
PLT189	Recall carburetor - effects of carburetor heat / heat control
PLT190	Recall carburetor ice - factors affecting / causing
PLT191	Recall carburetors - types / components / operating principles / characteristics
PLT192	Recall clouds - types / formation / resulting weather
PLT193	Recall cockpit voice recorder (CVR) - operating principles / characteristics / testing
PLT194	Recall collision avoidance - scanning techniques
PLR195	Recall collision avoidance - TCAS
PLT196	Recall communications - ATIS broadcasts
PLT197	Recall Coriolis effect
PLT198	Recall course / heading - effects of wind
PLT199	Recall cyclic control pressure - characteristics
PLT200	Recall dead reckoning - calculations / charts
PLT201	Recall departure procedures - ODP / SID
PLT202	Recall DME - characteristics / accuracy / indications / Arc
PLT203	Recall earth`s atmosphere - layers / characteristics / solar energy
PLT204	Recall effective communication - basic elements
PLT205	Recall effects of alcohol on the body
PLT206	Recall effects of temperature - density altitude / icing

Code	Learning Statement
PLT207	Recall electrical system - components / operating principles / characteristics
PLT208	Recall emergency conditions / procedures
PLT209	Recall engine pressure ratio - EPR
PLT210	Recall engine shutdown - normal / abnormal / emergency / precautions
PLT211	Recall evaluation testing characteristics
PLT212	Recall fire extinguishing systems - components / operating principles / characteristics
PLT213	Recall flight characteristics - longitudinal stability / instability
PLT214	Recall flight characteristics - structural / wing design
PLT215	Recall flight instruments - magnetic compass
PLT216	Recall flight instruments - total energy compensators
PLT217	Recall flight maneuvers - quick stop
PLT218	Recall flight operations - common student errors
PLT219	Recall flight operations - maneuvers
PLT220	Recall flight operations - night and high altitude operations
PLT221	Recall flight operations - takeoff / landing maneuvers
PLT222	Recall flight operations - takeoff procedures
PLT223	Recall flight operations multiengine - engine inoperative procedures
PLT224	Recall flight plan - IFR
PLT225	Recall flight plan - requirements
PLT226	Recall fog - types / formation / resulting weather
PLT227	Recall FOI techniques - integrated flight instruction
PLT228	Recall FOI techniques - lesson plans
PLT229	Recall FOI techniques - professionalism
PLT230	Recall FOI techniques - responsibilities
PLT231	Recall FOI techniques / human behavior - anxiety / fear / stress
PLT232	Recall FOI techniques / human behavior - dangerous tendencies
PLT233	Recall FOI techniques / human behavior - defense mechanisms
PLT234	Recall forces acting on aircraft - 3 axis intersect
PLT235	Recall forces acting on aircraft - aerodynamics
PLT236	Recall forces acting on aircraft - airfoil / center of pressure / mean camber line
PLT237	Recall forces acting on aircraft - airspeed / air density / lift / drag
PLT238	Recall forces acting on aircraft - aspect ratio
PLT239	Recall forces acting on aircraft - buoyancy / drag / gravity / thrust
PLT240	Recall forces acting on aircraft - CG / flight characteristics
PLT241	Recall forces acting on aircraft - drag / gravity / thrust / lift
PLT242	Recall forces acting on aircraft - lift / drag / thrust / weight / stall / limitations
PLT243	Recall forces acting on aircraft - propeller / torque
PLT244	Recall forces acting on aircraft - stability / controllability
PLT245	Recall forces acting on aircraft - stalls / spins
PLT246	Recall forces acting on aircraft - steady state climb / flight
PLT247	Recall forces acting on aircraft - thrust / drag / weight / lift
PLT248	Recall forces acting on aircraft - turns
PLT249	Recall fuel - air mixture
PLT250	Recall fuel - types / characteristics / contamination / fueling / defueling / precautions
PLT251	Recall fuel characteristics / contaminants / additives / leaks

Code	Learning Statement
PLT252	Recall fuel dump system - components / methods
PLT253	Recall fuel system - components / operating principles / characteristics
PLT254	Recall fuel tank - components / operating principles / characteristics
PLT255	Recall fueling procedures - safety / grounding / calculating volume
PLT256	Recall glider performance - effect of loading
PLT257	Recall glider performance - speed / distance / ballast / lift / drag
PLT258	Recall ground reference maneuvers - ground track diagram
PLT259	Recall ground resonance - conditions to occur
PLT260	Recall gyroplane - aerodynamics / rotor systems
PLT261	Recall hail - characteristics / hazards
PLT262	Recall hazardous material - reports / transportation procedures / labeling
PLT263	Recall hazardous weather - fog / icing / turbulence
PLT264	Recall helicopter approach - settling with power
PLT265	Recall helicopter takeoff / landing - ground resonance action required
PLT266	Recall high lift devices - characteristics / functions
PLT267	Recall hot air balloon - weigh-off procedure
PLT268	Recall hovering - aircraft performance / tendencies
PLT269	Recall human behavior - defense mechanism
PLT270	Recall human behavior - social / self fulfillment / physical
PLT271	Recall human factors (ADM) - judgment
PLT272	Recall human factors - stress management
PLT273	Recall hydraulic systems - components / operating principles / characteristics
PLT274	Recall icing - formation / characteristics
PLT275	Recall ILS - indications / HSI
PLT276	Recall ILS - indications / OBS / CDI
PLT277	Recall ILS - marker beacon / indicator lights / codes
PLT278	Recall indicating systems - airspeed/angle of attack/attitude/heading/manifold pressure/synchro/EGT
PLT279	Recall Inertial Navigation System principles
PLT280	Recall inflight illusions - causes / sources
PLT281	Recall information in an Airport Facility Directory
PLT282	Recall information in the certificate holder`s manual
PLT283	Recall information on a Constant Pressure Analysis Chart
PLT284	Recall information on a Forecast Winds and Temperatures Aloft (FD)
PLT285	Recall information on a Height Velocity Diagram
PLT286	Recall information on a Significant Weather Prognostic Chart
PLT287	Recall information on a Surface Analysis Chart
PLT288	Recall information on a Terminal Aerodrome Forecast (TAF)
PLT289	Recall information on a Weather Depiction Chart
PLT290	Recall information on AIRMETS / SIGMETS
PLT291	Recall information on an Aviation Area Forecast (FA)
PLT292	Recall information on an Instrument Approach Procedures (IAP)
PLT293	Recall information on an Instrument Departure Procedure Chart
PLT294	Recall information on Inflight Aviation Weather Advisories
PLT295	Recall instructor techniques - obstacles / planning / activities / outcome
PLT296	Recall instrument procedures - holding / circling

Code	Learning Statement
PLT297	Recall instrument procedures - unusual attitude / unusual attitude recovery
PLT298	Recall instrument procedures - VFR on top
PLT300	Recall instrument/navigation system checks/inspections - limits / tuning / identifying / logging
PLT301	Recall inversion layer - characteristics
PLT302	Recall jet stream - types / characteristics
PLT303	Recall L/D ratio
PLT304	Recall launch procedures
PLT305	Recall leading edge devices - types / effect / purpose / operation
PLT306	Recall learning process - levels of learning / transfer of learning / incidental learning
PLT307	Recall learning process - memory / fact / recall
PLT308	Recall learning process - principles of learning elements
PLT309	Recall load factor - angle of bank
PLT310	Recall load factor - characteristics
PLT311	Recall load factor - effect of airspeed
PLT312	Recall load factor - maneuvering / stall speed
PLT313	Recall loading - limitations
PLT314	Recall longitudinal axis - aerodynamics / center of gravity / direction of motion
PLT315	Recall Machmeter - principles / functions
PLT316	Recall meteorology - severe weather watch (WW)
PLT317	Recall microburst - characteristics / hazards
PLT318	Recall minimum fuel advisory
PLT319	Recall navigation - celestial
PLT320	Recall navigation - true north / magnetic north
PLT321	Recall navigation - types of landing systems
PLT322	Recall navigation - VOR / NAV system
PLT323	Recall NOTAMS - classes / information / distribution
PLT324	Recall oil system - types / components / functions
PLT325	Recall operations manual - transportation of prisoner
PLT326	Recall oxygen system - components / operating principles / characteristics
PLT327	Recall oxygen system - install / inspect / repair / service / precautions / leaks
PLT328	Recall performance planning - aircraft loading
PLT329	Recall physiological factors - cabin pressure
PLT330	Recall physiological factors - cause / effects of hypoxia
PLT331	Recall physiological factors - effects of scuba diving / smoking
PLT332	Recall physiological factors - hyperventilation
PLT333	Recall physiological factors - night vision
PLT334	Recall physiological factors - spatial disorientation
PLT335	Recall pilotage - calculations
PLT336	Recall pitch control - collective / cyclic
PLT337	Recall pitot-static system - components / operating principles / characteristics
PLT338	Recall pneumatic system - operation
PLT340	Recall positive exchange of flight controls
PLT341	Recall power settling - characteristics
PLT342	Recall powerplant - controlling engine temperature
PLT343	Recall powerplant - operating principles / operational characteristics / inspecting

Code	Learning Statement
PLT344	Recall precipitation - types / characteristics
PLT345	Recall pressure altitude
PLT346	Recall primary flight controls - types / purpose / functionality
PLT347	Recall principles of flight - critical engine
PLT348	Recall principles of flight - turns
PLT349	Recall procedures for confined areas
PLT350	Recall propeller operations - constant / variable speed
PLT351	Recall propeller system - types / components / operating principles / characteristics
PLT352	Recall purpose / operation of a stabilizer
PLT353	Recall Radar Summary Chart
PLT354	Recall radio - GPS / RNAV / RAIM
PLT355	Recall radio - HSI
PLT356	Recall radio - ILS / compass locator
PLT357	Recall radio - ILS / LDA
PLT358	Recall radio - LOC / ILS
PLT359	Recall radio - LORAN
PLT360	Recall radio - Microwave Landing System
PLT361	Recall radio - SDF / ILS
PLT362	Recall radio - VHF / Direction Finding
PLT363	Recall radio - VOR / VOT
PLT364	Recall radio system - licence requirements / frequencies
PLT365	Recall reciprocating engine - components / operating principles / characteristics
PLT366	Recall regulations - accident / incident reporting and preserving wreckage
PLT367	Recall regulations - additional equipment/operating requirements large transport aircraft
PLT368	Recall regulations - admission to flight deck
PLT369	Recall regulations - aerobatic flight requirements
PLT370	Recall regulations - Air Traffic Control authorization / clearances
PLT371	Recall regulations - Aircraft Category / Class
PLT372	Recall regulations - aircraft inspection / records / expiration
PLT373	Recall regulations - aircraft operating limitations
PLT374	Recall regulations - aircraft owner / operator responsibilities
PLT375	Recall regulations - aircraft return to service
PLT376	Recall regulations - airspace special use / TFRS
PLT377	Recall regulations - airworthiness certificates / requirements / responsibilities
PLT378	Recall regulations - Airworthiness Directives
PLT379	Recall regulations - alternate airport requirements
PLT380	Recall regulations - alternate airport weather minima
PLT381	Recall regulations - altimeter settings
PLT382	Recall regulations - approach minima
PLT383	Recall regulations - basic flight rules
PLT384	Recall regulations - briefing of passengers
PLT385	Recall regulations - cargo in passenger compartment
PLT386	Recall regulations - certificate issuance / renewal
PLT387	Recall regulations - change of address
PLT388	Recall regulations - cockpit voice recorder / flight data recorder(s)

Code	Learning Statement
PLT389	Recall regulations - commercial operation requirements / conditions / OpSpecs
PLT390	Recall regulations - communications enroute
PLT391	Recall regulations - communications failure
PLT392	Recall regulations - compliance with local regulations
PLT393	Recall regulations - controlled / restricted airspace - requirements
PLT394	Recall regulations - declaration of an emergency
PLT395	Recall regulations - definitions
PLT396	Recall regulations - departure alternate airport
PLT397	Recall regulations - destination airport visibility
PLT398	Recall regulations - dispatch
PLT399	Recall regulations - display / inspection of licences and certificates
PLT400	Recall regulations - documents to be carried on aircraft during flight
PLT401	Recall regulations - dropping / aerial application / towing restrictions
PLT402	Recall regulations - ELT requirements
PLT403	Recall regulations - emergency deviation from regulations
PLT404	Recall regulations - emergency equipment
PLT405	Recall regulations - equipment / instrument / certificate requirements
PLT406	Recall regulations - equipment failure
PLT407	Recall regulations - experience / training requirements
PLT408	Recall regulations - fire extinguisher requirements
PLT409	Recall regulations - flight / duty time
PLT410	Recall regulations - flight engineer qualifications / privileges / responsibilities
PLT411	Recall regulations - flight instructor limitations / qualifications
PLT412	Recall regulations - flight release
PLT413	Recall regulations - fuel requirements
PLT414	Recall regulations - general right-of-way rules
PLT415	Recall regulations - IFR flying
PLT416	Recall regulations - immediate notification
PLT417	Recall regulations - individual flotation devices
PLT418	Recall regulations - instructor demonstrations / authorizations
PLT419	Recall regulations - instructor requirements / responsibilities
PLT420	Recall regulations - instrument approach procedures
PLT421	Recall regulations - instrument flight rules
PLT422	Recall regulations - intermediate airport authorizations
PLT423	Recall regulations - knowledge and skill test checks
PLT424	Recall regulations - limits on autopilot usage
PLT425	Recall regulations - maintenance reports / records / entries
PLT426	Recall regulations - maintenance requirements
PLT427	Recall regulations - medical certificate requirements / validity
PLT428	Recall regulations - minimum equipment list
PLT429	Recall regulations - minimum flight / navigation instruments
PLT430	Recall regulations - minimum safe / flight altitude
PLT431	Recall regulations - operating near other aircraft
PLT432	Recall regulations - operational control functions
PLT433	Recall regulations - operational flight plan requirements

Code	Learning Statement
PLT434	Recall regulations - operational procedures for a controlled airport
PLT435	Recall regulations - operational procedures for an uncontrolled airport
PLT436	Recall regulations - operations manual
PLT437	Recall regulations - overwater operations
PLT438	Recall regulations - oxygen requirements
PLT439	Recall regulations - persons authorized to perform maintenance
PLT440	Recall regulations - Pilot / Crew duties and responsibilities
PLT441	Recall regulations - pilot briefing
PLT442	Recall regulations - pilot currency requirements
PLT443	Recall regulations - pilot qualifications / privileges / responsibilities
PLT444	Recall regulations - pilot-in-command authority / responsibility
PLT445	Recall regulations - preflight requirements
PLT446	Recall regulations - preventative maintenance
PLT447	Recall regulations - privileges / limitations of medical certificates
PLT448	Recall regulations - privileges / limitations of pilot certificates
PLT449	Recall regulations - proficiency check requirements
PLT450	Recall regulations - qualifications / duty time
PLT451	Recall regulations - ratings issued / experience requirements / limitations
PLT452	Recall regulations - re-dispatch
PLT453	Recall regulations - records retention for domestic / flag air carriers
PLT454	Recall regulations - required aircraft / equipment inspections
PLT455	Recall regulations - requirements of a flight plan release
PLT456	Recall regulations - runway requirements
PLT457	Recall regulations - student pilot endorsements / other endorsements
PLT458	Recall regulations - submission / revision of Policy and Procedure Manuals
PLT459	Recall regulations - takeoff procedures / minimums
PLT460	Recall regulations - training programs
PLT461	Recall regulations - use of aircraft lights
PLT462	Recall regulations - use of microphone / megaphone / interphone
PLT463	Recall regulations - use of narcotics / drugs / intoxicating liquor
PLT464	Recall regulations - use of safety belts / harnesses (crew member)
PLT465	Recall regulations - use of seats / safety belts / harnesses (passenger)
PLT466	Recall regulations - V speeds
PLT467	Recall regulations - visual flight rules and limitations
PLT468	Recall regulations - Visual Meteorological Conditions (VMC)
PLT469	Recall regulations - weather radar
PLT470	Recall rotor system - types / components / operating principles / characteristics
PLT471	Recall rotorcraft transmission - components / operating principles / characteristics
PLT472	Recall rotorcraft vibration - characteristics / sources
PLT473	Recall secondary flight controls - types / purpose / functionality
PLT474	Recall soaring - normal procedures
PLT475	Recall squall lines - formation / characteristics / resulting weather
PLT476	Recall stabilizer - purpose / operation
PLT477	Recall stalls - characteristics / factors / recovery / precautions
PLT478	Recall starter / ignition system - types / components / operating principles / characteristics

Code	Learning Statement
PLT479	Recall starter system - starting procedures
PLT480	Recall static/dynamic stability/instability - characteristics
PLT481	Recall student evaluation - learning process
PLT482	Recall student evaluation - written tests / oral quiz / critiques
PLT483	Recall supercharger - characteristics / operation
PLT484	Recall symbols - chart / navigation
PLT485	Recall taxiing / crosswind / techniques
PLT486	Recall taxiing / takeoff - techniques / procedures
PLT487	Recall teaching methods - demonstration / performance
PLT488	Recall teaching methods - group / guided discussion / lecture
PLT489	Recall teaching methods - known to unknown
PLT490	Recall teaching methods - motivation / student feelings of insecurity
PLT491	Recall teaching methods - organizing material / course of training
PLT492	Recall temperature - effects on weather formations
PLT493	Recall the dynamics of frost / ice / snow formation on an aircraft
PLT494	Recall thermals - types / characteristics / formation / locating / maneuvering / corrective actions
PLT495	Recall thunderstorms - types / characteristics / formation / hazards
PLT496	Recall towrope - strength / safety links / positioning
PLT497	Recall transponder - codes / operations / usage
PLT498	Recall Transportation Security Regulations
PLT499	Recall turbine engines - components / operational characteristics / associated instruments
PLT500	Recall turboprop engines - components / operational characteristics
PLT501	Recall turbulence - types / characteristics / reporting / corrective actions
PLT502	Recall universal signals - hand / light / visual
PLT503	Recall use of narcotics / drugs / intoxicating liquor
PLT504	Recall use of training aids - types / function / purpose
PLT505	Recall use of training aids - usefulness / simplicity / compatibility
PLT506	Recall V speeds - maneuvering / flap extended / gear extended
PLT507	Recall VOR - indications / VOR / VOT / CDI
PLT508	Recall VOR/altimeter/transponder checks - identification / tuning / identifying / logging
PLT509	Recall wake turbulence - characteristics / avoidance techniques
PLT510	Recall weather - causes / formation
PLT511	Recall weather associated with frontal activity / air masses
PLT512	Recall weather conditions - temperature / moisture / dewpoint
PLT513	Recall weather information - TWEB broadcasts
PLT514	Recall weather reporting systems - briefings / forecasts / reports
PLT515	Recall weather services - EFAS / TIBS / WFO / AFSS / HIWAS
PLT516	Recall winds - types / characteristics
PLT517	Recall winds associated with high / low-pressure systems
PLT518	Recall windshear - characteristics / hazards / power management
PLT519	Recall wing spoilers - purpose / operation
PLT520	Calculate density altitude
PLT521	Recall helicopter takeoff / landing – slope operations
PLT522	Recall helicopter – Pinnacle / Ridgeline operations
PLT523	Recall vortex generators - purpose / effects / aerodynamics

APPENDIX B

EXAMS AND ANSWER KEYS

Airplane Private Pilot
End-of-Course Examination "A"

Note:
The numbers on the left side of each column correspond to the numbers on the exam answer sheet. The numbers on the right side of each column correspond to the question number in the Question Bank.

ON ANSWER SHEET FOR ITEM NUMBER	ANSWER QUESTION NUMBER	ON ANSWER SHEET FOR ITEM NUMBER	ANSWER QUESTION NUMBER	ON ANSWER SHEET FOR ITEM NUMBER	ANSWER QUESTION NUMBER
1	25	18	234	35	422
2	31	19	267	36	435
3	48	20	271	37	443
4	58	21	272	38	480
5	70	22	276	39	496
6	78	23	278	40	508
7	91	24	280	41	531
8	99	25	309	42	533
9	114	26	315	43	535
10	122	27	334	44	577
11	124	28	343	45	580
12	149	29	345	46	605
13	164	30	370	47	627
14	174	31	377	48	718
15	195	32	386	49	740
16	207	33	400	50	748
17	214	34	420		

Airplane Private Pilot
End-of-Course Examination "B"

Note:
The numbers on the left side of each column correspond to the numbers on the exam answer sheet. The numbers on the right side of each column correspond to the question number in the Question Bank.

ON ANSWER SHEET FOR ITEM NUMBER	ANSWER QUESTION NUMBER	ON ANSWER SHEET FOR ITEM NUMBER	ANSWER QUESTION NUMBER	ON ANSWER SHEET FOR ITEM NUMBER	ANSWER QUESTION NUMBER
1	12	18	198	35	455
2	16	19	202	36	479
3	21	20	215	37	491
4	23	21	223	38	510
5	29	22	227	39	557
6	54	23	236	40	581
7	60	24	273	41	583
8	63	25	289	42	590
9	68	26	326	43	592
10	79	27	344	44	595
11	84	28	353	45	609
12	88	29	375	46	615
13	115	30	385	47	640
14	144	31	393	48	706
15	146	32	409	49	722
16	162	33	420	50	753
17	195	34	441		

Helicopter Private Pilot Stage I Examination

Note:
The numbers on the left side of each column correspond to the numbers on the exam answer sheet. The numbers on the right side of each column correspond to the question number in the Question Bank.

ON ANSWER SHEET FOR ITEM NUMBER	ANSWER QUESTION NUMBER	ON ANSWER SHEET FOR ITEM NUMBER	ANSWER QUESTION NUMBER	ON ANSWER SHEET FOR ITEM NUMBER	ANSWER QUESTION NUMBER
1	3	16	278	31	636
2	11	17	290	32	717
3	16	18	307	33	753
4	18	19	317	34	755
5	25	20	318	35	761
6	32	21	344	36	768
7	64	22	345	37	780
8	80	23	356	38	785
9	91	24	374	39	788
10	154	25	378	40	789
11	159	26	391	41	792
12	231	27	479	42	794
13	233	28	505	43	796
14	241	29	544	44	801
15	277	30	631	45	804

Helicopter Private Pilot Stage II Examination

Note:
The numbers on the left side of each column correspond to the numbers on the exam answer sheet. The numbers on the right side of each column correspond to the question number in the Question Bank.

ON ANSWER SHEET FOR ITEM NUMBER	ANSWER QUESTION NUMBER	ON ANSWER SHEET FOR ITEM NUMBER	ANSWER QUESTION NUMBER	ON ANSWER SHEET FOR ITEM NUMBER	ANSWER QUESTION NUMBER
1	195	11	432	21	546
2	196	12	433	22	561
3	216	13	437	23	563
4	226	14	441	24	565
5	408	15	458	25	572
6	410	16	462	26	577
7	418	17	464	27	578
8	419	18	465	28	585
9	422	19	472	29	777
10	423	20	530	30	783

Helicopter Private Pilot Stage III Examination

Note:
The numbers on the left side of each column correspond to the numbers on the exam answer sheet. The numbers on the right side of each column correspond to the question number in the Question Bank.

ON ANSWER SHEET FOR ITEM NUMBER	ANSWER QUESTION NUMBER	ON ANSWER SHEET FOR ITEM NUMBER	ANSWER QUESTION NUMBER	ON ANSWER SHEET FOR ITEM NUMBER	ANSWER QUESTION NUMBER
1	203	10	596	19	621
2	310	11	597	20	623
3	333	12	599	21	644
4	528	13	600	22	648
5	533	14	601	23	693
6	547	15	602	24	695
7	552	16	604	25	773
8	591	17	605		
9	592	18	618		

Helicopter Private Pilot End-of-Course Examination

Note:
The numbers on the left side of each column correspond to the numbers on the exam answer sheet. The numbers on the right side of each column correspond to the question number in the Question Bank.

ON ANSWER SHEET FOR ITEM NUMBER	ANSWER QUESTION NUMBER	ON ANSWER SHEET FOR ITEM NUMBER	ANSWER QUESTION NUMBER	ON ANSWER SHEET FOR ITEM NUMBER	ANSWER QUESTION NUMBER
1	1	21	413	41	691
2	17	22	416	42	747
3	52	23	425	43	754
4	61	24	457	44	756
5	86	25	463	45	758
6	94	26	527	46	762
7	151	27	531	47	770
8	197	28	534	48	772
9	204	29	554	49	776
10	207	30	568	50	779
11	214	31	574	51	784
12	254	32	589	52	786
13	273	33	594	53	787
14	314	34	620	54	789
15	316	35	622	55	791
16	349	36	637	56	793
17	352	37	643	57	795
18	362	38	650	58	797
19	376	39	678	59	799
20	395	40	684	60	800

Private Pilot Airman Knowledge Test Question Bank Answers

1. – B	69. – C	137. – C	205. – C	273. – C	341. – B
2. – B	70. – B	138. – C	206. – A	274. – B	342. – C
3. – A	71. – C	139. – A	207. – C	275. – C	343. – A
4. – B	72. – C	140. – C	208. – A	276. – B	344. – C
5. – A	73. – B	141. – B	209. – B	277. – C	345. – C
6. – B	74. – C	142. – A	210. – B	278. – C	346. – A
7. – B	75. – A	143. – C	211. – C	279. – A	347. – A
8. – A	76. – C	144. – A	212. – C	280. – B	348. – C
9. – B	77. – C	145. – A	213. – B	281. – B	349. – B
10. – C	78. – C	146. – A	214. – B	282. – C	350. – A
11. – A	79. – B	147. – A	215. – C	283. – C	351. – A
12. – A	80. – C	148. – C	216. – B	284. – B	352. – B
13. – B	81. – C	149. – B	217. – C	285. – C	353. – C
14. – B	82. – C	150. – A	218. – C	286. – A	354. – B
15. – A	83. – B	151. – C	219. – B	287. – C	355. – A
16. – A	84. – A	152. – B	220. – C	288. – B	356. – A
17. – C	85. – C	153. – A	221. – B	289. – A	357. – A
18. – A	86. – A	154. – C	222. – C	290. – C	358. – C
19. – C	87. – C	155. – B	223. – B	291. – C	359. – A
20. – B	88. – B	156. – B	224. – B	292. – B	360. – C
21. – B	89. – C	157. – B	225. – B	293. – B	361. – B
22. – A	90. – C	158. – B	226. – C	294. – A	362. – A
23. – C	91. – B	159. – B	227. – B	295. – C	363. – A
24. – A	92. – A	160. – A	228. – A	296. – A	364. – C
25. – C	93. – C	161. – C	229. – A	297. – A	365. – B
26. – C	94. – B	162. – B	230. – C	298. – B	366. – B
27. – A	95. – B	163. – C	231. – B	299. – C	367. – C
28. – B	96. – C	164. – B	232. – A	300. – B	368. – A
29. – B	97. – B	165. – B	233. – B	301. – C	369. – A
30. – A	98. – B	166. – B	234. – A	302. – C	370. – C
31. – A	99. – A	167. – C	235. – A	303. – A	371. – A
32. – C	100. – A	168. – B	236. – C	304. – A	372. – C
33. – C	101. – B	169. – B	237. – A	305. – B	373. – B
34. – A	102. – A	170. – B	238. – B	306. – C	374. – C
35. – A	103. – A	171. – B	239. – B	307. – B	375. – C
36. – A	104. – C	172. – B	240. – B	308. – B	376. – C
37. – A	105. – A	173. – A	241. – A	309. – C	377. – B
38. – B	106. – C	174. – C	242. – B	310. – B	378. – B
39. – B	107. – A	175. – C	243. – A	311. – C	379. – C
40. – A	108. – A	176. – C	244. – A	312. – B	380. – A
41. – B	109. – B	177. – B	245. – C	313. – C	381. – C
42. – C	110. – B	178. – A	246. – C	314. – A	382. – B
43. – C	111. – C	179. – C	247. – B	315. – A	383. – C
44. – A	112. – B	180. – C	248. – C	316. – A	384. – C
45. – B	113. – C	181. – A	249. – B	317. – A	385. – C
46. – A	114. – B	182. – B	250. – B	318. – A	386. – C
47. – B	115. – A	183. – C	251. – A	319. – C	387. – A
48. – C	116. – B	184. – A	252. – C	320. – C	388. – B
49. – C	117. – B	185. – A	253. – B	321. – A	389. – B
50. – C	118. – A	186. – A	254. – A	322. – A	390. – B
51. – C	119. – C	187. – B	255. – C	323. – C	391. – A
52. – A	120. – A	188. – B	256. – C	324. – B	392. – B
53. – B	121. – A	189. – C	257. – B	325. – A	393. – A
54. – C	122. – B	190. – B	258. – B	326. – C	394. – A
55. – A	123. – B	191. – A	259. – A	327. – C	395. – B
56. – A	124. – C	192. – B	260. – B	328. – C	396. – B
57. – B	125. – C	193. – C	261. – C	329. – A	397. – C
58. – B	126. – B	194. – C	262. – A	330. – A	398. – A
59. – B	127. – B	195. – A	263. – B	331. – C	399. – C
60. – B	128. – B	196. – B	264. – C	332. – B	400. – C
61. – C	129. – A	197. – C	265. – A	333. – B	401. – A
62. – C	130. – A	198. – C	266. – C	334. – B	402. – C
63. – C	131. – C	199. – B	267. – B	335. – C	403. – B
64. – C	132. – B	200. – B	268. – B	336. – B	404. – A
65. – A	133. – B	201. – A	269. – B	337. – A	405. – B
66. – C	134. – A	202. – B	270. – A	338. – B	406. – A
67. – C	135. – A	203. – B	271. – C	339. – C	407. – C
68. – C	136. – B	204. – A	272. – C	340. – A	408. – C

409. – B	477. – B	545. – B	613. – C	681. – C	749. – B
410. – A	478. – C	546. – C	614. – C	682. – C	750. – A
411. – B	479. – B	547. – C	615. – A	683. – A	751. – B
412. – B	480. – B	548. – A	616. – A	684. – B	752. – C
413. – A	481. – C	549. – B	617. – B	685. – B	753. – C
414. – C	482. – B	550. – B	618. – B	686. – B	754. – A
415. – A	483. – B	551. – A	619. – B	687. – B	755. – C
416. – A	484. – C	552. – B	620. – C	688. – C	756. – B
417. – C	485. – B	553. – A	621. – C	689. – B	757. – A
418. – A	486. – C	554. – A	622. – A	690. – B	758. – B
419. – C	487. – C	555. – A	623. – B	691. – A	759. – C
420. – C	488. – C	556. – A	624. – C	692. – A	760. – C
421. – A	489. – B	557. – B	625. – A	693. – C	761. – B
422. – B	490. – A	558. – C	626. – A	694. – B	762. – C
423. – A	491. – C	559. – B	627. – C	695. – C	763. – C
424. – C	492. – B	560. – B	628. – A	696. – C	764. – B
425. – A	493. – A	561. – A	629. – B	697. – A	765. – B
426. – A	494. – B	562. – A	630. – B	698. – C	766. – C
427. – B	495. – B	563. – B	631. – C	699. – B	767. – B
428. – B	496. – C	564. – B	632. – C	700. – A	768. – C
429. – A	497. – B	565. – B	633. – B	701. – B	769. – B
430. – A	498. – B	566. – A	634. – C	702. – C	770. – A
431. – C	499. – B	567. – B	635. – C	703. – B	771. – A
432. – C	500. – B	568. – A	636. – C	704. – B	772. – C
433. – B	501. – A	569. – C	637. – C	705. – A	773. – A
434. – A	502. – A	570. – C	638. – C	706. – A	774. – C
435. – C	503. – B	571. – B	639. – B	707. – B	775. – B
436. – A	504. – A	572. – A	640. – C	708. – B	776. – B
437. – C	505. – C	573. – C	641. – C	709. – A	777. – C
438. – B	506. – B	574. – C	642. – A	710. – B	778. – B
439. – B	507. – A	575. – C	643. – C	711. – C	779. – B
440. – A	508. – C	576. – C	644. – C	712. – B	780. – C
441. – C	509. – A	577. – B	645. – A	713. – C	781. – A
442. – B	510. – B	578. – C	646. – C	714. – B	782. – C
443. – A	511. – C	579. – A	647. – C	715. – B	783. – C
444. – A	512. – B	580. – C	648. – B	716. – C	784. – A
445. – A	513. – B	581. – B	649. – A	717. – B	785. – A
446. – C	514. – A	582. – A	650. – A	718. – B	786. – C
447. – C	515. – B	583. – B	651. – A	719. – C	787. – C
448. – C	516. – A	584. – C	652. – C	720. – A	788. – B
449. – A	517. – B	585. – B	653. – C	721. – C	789. – A
450. – A	518. – C	586. – C	654. – A	722. – B	790. – A
451. – C	519. – A	587. – B	655. – C	723. – B	791. – B
452. – A	520. – C	588. – B	656. – B	724. – B	792. – C
453. – A	521. – B	589. – B	657. – A	725. – A	793. – B
454. – A	522. – C	590. – A	658. – A	726. – A	794. – C
455. – B	523. – A	591. – C	659. – C	727. – B	795. – B
456. – A	524. – C	592. – A	660. – A	728. – B	796. – A
457. – B	525. – A	593. – A	661. – A	729. – B	797. – B
458. – A	526. – C	594. – C	662. – C	730. – B	798. – A
459. – B	527. – C	595. – C	663. – B	731. – B	799. – B
460. – A	528. – B	596. – B	664. – C	732. – C	800. – A
461. – B	529. – B	597. – A	665. – C	733. – A	801. – C
462. – A	530. – C	598. – A	666. – B	734. – C	802. – B
463. – C	531. – B	599. – A	667. – A	735. – B	803. – C
464. – C	532. – C	600. – B	668. – C	736. – B	804. – C
465. – C	533. – B	601. – A	669. – C	737. – B	805. – B
466. – A	534. – C	602. – C	670. – A	738. – B	
467. – A	535. – A	603. – B	671. – B	739. – C	
468. – A	536. – A	604. – A	672. – B	740. – C	
469. – B	537. – C	605. – B	673. – C	741. – A	
470. – C	538. – A	606. – A	674. – C	742. – B	
471. – C	539. – B	607. – A	675. – C	743. – B	
472. – C	540. – C	608. – C	676. – C	744. – C	
473. – A	541. – B	609. – C	677. – B	745. – A	
474. – A	542. – C	610. – C	678. – A	746. – C	
475. – C	543. – C	611. – B	679. – B	747. – A	
476. – A	544. – B	612. – C	680. – B	748. – C	

AIRPLANE PRIVATE PILOT END-OF-COURSE EXAMINATION "A"

#	Ans	#	Ans
1	C	26	A
2	A	27	B
3	C	28	A
4	B	29	C
5	B	30	C
6	C	31	B
7	B	32	C
8	A	33	C
9	B	34	C
10	B	35	B
11	C	36	C
12	B	37	A
13	B	38	B
14	C	39	C
15	A	40	C
16	C	41	B
17	B	42	B
18	A	43	A
19	B	44	B
20	C	45	C
21	C	46	B
22	B	47	C
23	C	48	B
24	B	49	C
25	C	50	C

AIRPLANE PRIVATE PILOT END-OF-COURSE EXAMINATION "B"

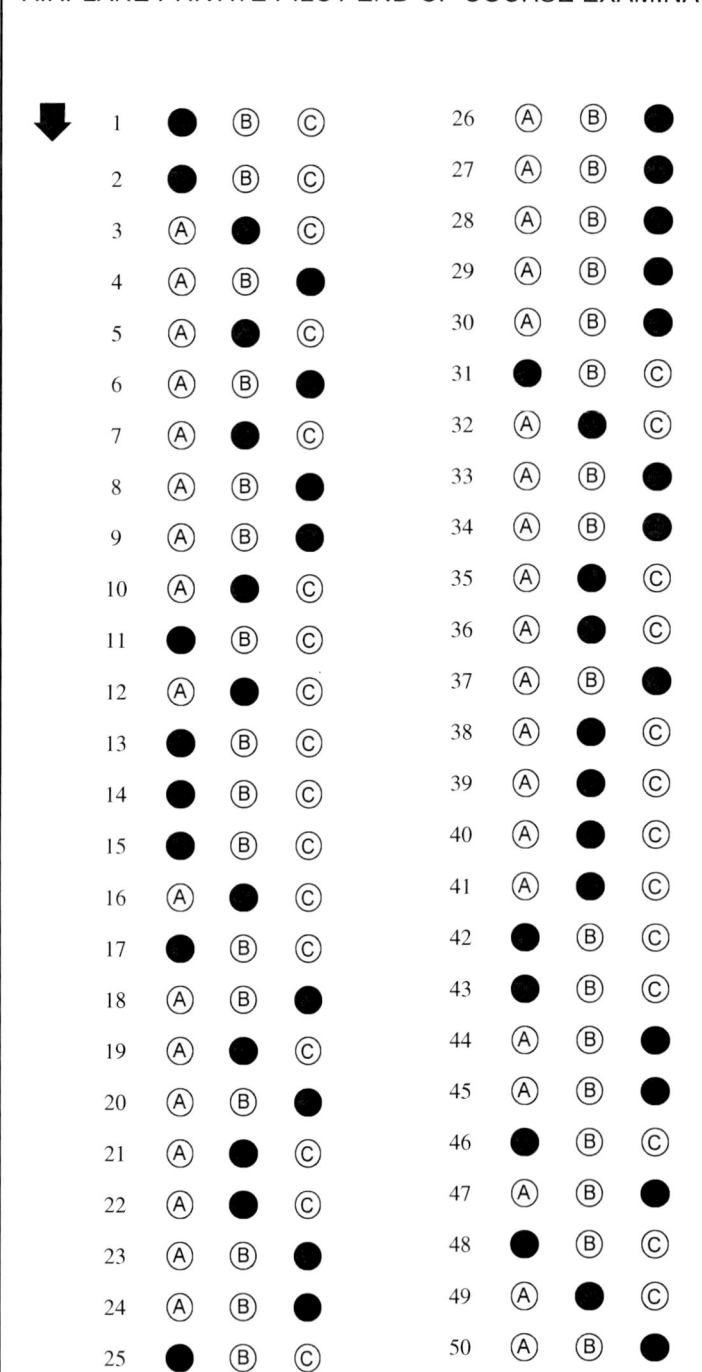

#	Answer	#	Answer
1	A	26	C
2	A	27	C
3	B	28	C
4	C	29	C
5	B	30	C
6	C	31	A
7	B	32	B
8	C	33	C
9	C	34	C
10	B	35	B
11	A	36	B
12	B	37	C
13	A	38	B
14	A	39	B
15	A	40	B
16	B	41	B
17	A	42	A
18	C	43	A
19	B	44	C
20	C	45	C
21	B	46	A
22	B	47	C
23	C	48	A
24	C	49	B
25	A	50	C